BFI FILM CLASS

. . . .

Rob White
SERIES EDITOR

Edward Buscombe, Colin MacCabe and David Meeker
SERIES CONSULTANTS

Launched in 1992, BFI Film Classics is a series of books that introduces, interprets and honours 360 landmark works of world cinema. The series includes a wide range of approaches and critical styles, reflecting the diverse ways we appreciate, analyse and enjoy great films.

Magnificently concentrated examples of flowing freeform critical poetry.
Uncut

A formidable body of work collectively generating some fascinating insights into the evolution of cinema.
Times Higher Education Supplement

The choice of authors is as judicious, eclectic and original as the choice of titles.
Positif

Estimable.
Boston Globe

We congratulate the BFI for responding to the need to restore an informed level of critical writing for the general cinephile.
Canadian Journal of Film Studies

Well written, impeccably researched and beautifully presented ... as a publishing venture, it is difficult to fault.
Film Ireland

FORTHCOMING IN 2002
. . . .

The Blue Angel
S. S. Prawer

I Know Where I'm Going!
Pam Cook

The Manchurian Candidate
Greil Marcus

Mother India
Gayatri Chatterjee

To Be or Not to Be
Peter Barnes

Vertigo
Charles Barr

BFI FILM CLASSICS

OCTOBER
Октябрь
. . . .

Richard Taylor

 Publishing

This book is dedicated to Giles,
a true friend indeed to a friend in need.

First published in 2002 by the
BRITISH FILM INSTITUTE
21 Stephen Street, London W1T 1LN

Copyright © Richard Taylor 2002

The British Film Institute
promotes greater understanding
and appreciation of, and
access to, film and moving image
culture in the UK.

British Library Cataloguing-in-Publication Data
A catalogue record for this book is available from the British Library

ISBN 0–85170–916–8

Series design by
Andrew Barron & Collis Clements Associates

Typeset in Fournier and Franklin Gothic by
D R Bungay Associates, Burghfield, Berks

Printed in Great Britain by Cromwell Press, Trowbridge, Wiltshire

CONTENTS

. . . .

ACKNOWLEDGMENTS AND
NOTE ON VERSIONS OF 'OCTOBER'

. . . .

I am grateful to Alan Finlayson, Dan Healey, Giles Howell and Rob White for their comments on earlier drafts of this book; and to Oksana Bulgakowa, Neil Edmunds, Julian Graffy, Dan Healey, Giles Howell, Jeffrey Richards, John Riley and Rashit Yangirov for assistance on particular points or with particular materials. Any remaining factual mistakes or errors of judgment are of course my own.

My greatest debt, however, is to Giles Howell, who quite literally saved this book from oblivion when that nightmare of all authors struck and the hard disk on my computer crashed.

. . . .

Eisenstein's third feature film was made under the title *October* (*Oktiabr'*). It was only when it was released in Germany that the title was changed to *Ten Days that Shook the World*, after John Reed's eye-witness account which was already well-known both inside and outside the Soviet Union. This was a purely commercial decision.

Of the versions of *October* currently available in the UK, that on DVD from Eureka is the most complete and has the most consistently high picture quality. However, when the film was transferred to DVD all the Russian intertitles were removed and replaced by translations into American English and the title of the film was inexplicably changed to *October 1917*. The new intertitles do not match the standard of the visual images and contain errors of translation, spelling and grammar. This is particularly unfortunate as the intertitles in Eisenstein's silent films play an important part in both the rhythm and the montage. For *October* all the intertitles were rendered in Russian in capital letters: this was partly to aid legibility for a semi-literate domestic mass audience and partly to avoid the question of whether 'God' should have a capital letter! The version that used to be distributed on video by Hendring did contain Russian titles with English subtitles but these are sometimes also inadequate or inaccurate. Wherever possible I have followed the Eureka DVD version, retaining the style and capitalisation but correcting the spelling, punctuation and grammatical errors and pointing out, where relevant, inconsistencies or inadequacies in the translations: in at least one case these are crucial to our understanding of Eisenstein's intentions.

The reader should also note that both versions are variants of the 1967 restoration, made to commemorate the fiftieth anniversary of the October Revolution by Eisenstein's long-time assistant Grigori Alexandrov, who had also been involved in the making of the original, but whose sensitivity to Eisenstein's original intentions sometimes leaves a considerable amount to be desired, as in the choice of music incorporated on the new soundtrack. A contemporary score for *October* was written by Edmund Meisel, whose music for *The Battleship Potemkin* (1925) contributed so much to that film's success in Germany. A 1930 obituary for Meisel claimed that he 'was a musician who in a way composed with his eyes, the only born film musician'.[1] Those who have seen either *October* or *Potemkin* with Meisel's score in live performance will almost certainly agree with this assessment but the *October* score has nonetheless not been recorded for any version of the film currently in distribution in the UK. Instead the added soundtrack for both video and DVD versions consists largely of a pastiche of the works of Dmitri Shostakovich. Although Shostakovich was a prolific composer of film music from the 1920s onwards, unlike Sergei Prokofiev, he *never* collaborated on a film score with Eisenstein.[2] Given Eisenstein's clearly expressed views on the role of sound in film, there can be absolutely no doubt that he would have viewed the addition of Shostakovich's music as at best a diversion.[3] This soundtrack is *not* authentic and readers in search of an authentic viewing experience are therefore best advised to view either DVD or video with the sound switched *off*.

In this book I have tried to transliterate Russian names in a user-friendly way; Russian words are rendered in accordance with the Library of Congress transliteration system.

'OCTOBER'

. . . .

Potemkin has something of the Greek temple, *October* is a little Baroque. There are parts of *October* which are purely experimental. Methods of intellectual film-making that I think will develop. For me, from the experimental point of view, *October* is more interesting.

Sergei Eisenstein[4]

Sergei Eisenstein first came to international prominence with his second feature film, *The Battleship Potemkin*, released in the Soviet Union in January 1926.[5] His reputation, both at home and abroad, ensured that he was one of the directors invited by the official Anniversary Commission in the autumn of 1926 to make a film to mark the tenth anniversary of the October 1917 Revolution. Among the other directors already recruited were Vsevolod Pudovkin (*The End of St Petersburg*), Dziga Vertov (*The Eleventh Year*), Esfir Shub (*The Great Way*) and Boris Barnet (*Moscow in October*). President Mikhail Kalinin handed Eisenstein a copy of John Reed's *Ten Days that Shook the World*, 'Here's a good book. Lenin thought highly of it. It might help you.' Eisenstein's assistant, Grigori Alexandrov, later recalled, 'Thus began an incredible cine-storm.'[6]

The decision to mark the tenth anniversary in this way built upon a long tradition of revolutionary celebration and carnival, dating back to the storming of the Bastille during the French Revolution and beyond – back to the bread and circuses of ancient Rome.[7]

In the Soviet context these festivals have been described as 'the behavioural dimension of ideology' and 'a means to structure and maintain power relations'.[8] In the spring of 1920, Anatoli Lunacharsky, People's Commissar for Enlightenment, argued:

There can be absolutely no doubt that the main artistic fruit of revolution has always been and always will be popular festivals.

Generally speaking, any genuine democracy strives naturally towards popular festival. Democracy presupposes the free life of the masses.

In order to acquire a sense of self the masses must outwardly manifest themselves and this is possible only when, in Robespierre's words, they become a spectacle unto themselves.

If the organised masses march to music, sing in unison or perform extensive gymnastic manoeuvres or dances, in other words, organising a kind of parade – not a military parade but one that is saturated with the ideological essence, the hopes, curses and all the other emotions of the people – then the others, the unorganised masses, lining all the streets and squares where the festival is taking place, will merge with the organised masses so that one can say: the whole people is manifesting its soul to itself.[9]

Specifically, one major inspiration for Eisenstein's own re-creation of October 1917 was the November 1920 re-enactment of *The Storming of the Winter Palace*, directed by Nikolai Evreinov, to celebrate the third anniversary of the October 1917 Revolution.[10] Evreinov later described some elements of the spectacle:

Silhouettes of those locked in battle were visible through the lighted windows of the Winter Palace ... The crackle of gunfire and rifle shots, the thunder of artillery guns ... two to three minutes of continuous din ... then a rocket soared up and everything instantly subsided only to be filled with the new sound of the 'Internationale' as sung by the forty-thousand chorus. As the lights in the windows were being extinguished, five-pointed red stars lit up and a huge red banner was raised above the Palace itself.[11]

The 8,000 participants in the 1920 spectacle far exceeded the number of people who had actually occupied the Palace three years before and, although rain reduced the size of the audience to around 100,000, this still represented a quarter of the city's population at that time. The audience was placed in Palace Square in the middle of the action and 150 spotlights were mounted on the roofs of surrounding buildings to highlight the action on two stages. When these lights were switched on, the power supply to parts of the city had to be switched off.

In practical as well as artistic terms, *The Storming of the Winter Palace* was to act as a model for *October*. Both offered a distillation of the same historical event, both contributed to the development of the foundation myth of the Soviet state. Crucially, both *improved* upon the original event for both artistic and political reasons, and neither Evreinov nor Eisenstein laid any claim to documentary authenticity or precise historical accuracy. As the libretto for the 1920 re-enactment put it:

> The tone of the historical events that serve as the raw material for the making of this spectacle is here reduced to a series of artistically

The Storming of the Winter Palace: the 1920 re-enactment

simplified moments and stage situations. The directors of the current spectacle did not give any consideration to a precise reproduction of the events that took place in the square in front of the Winter Palace three years ago. They did not, and indeed could not, because theatre was never meant to serve as the minute-taker of history.[12]

Festivals like this were designed to create a sense of identification between the audience and the event re-enacted through the spectacle itself and the act of collective memory that it both embodied and provoked. But, as James von Geldern has argued: 'A festival is not a neutral or "transparent" system; it is an artistic system in and out of itself, with its own rules of aesthetic construction that it imposes on the material at hand. In this process remembered events are changed.'[13] This is especially true when the memory of remembered events acquires its own momentum in what he calls a 'reformation of recollection'. One of the consultants for both re-enactments was Nikolai Podvoisky. He had been one of those in charge of the occupation of the Winter Palace in 1917 and in 1927 was to be both the chairman of the Anniversary Commission and a consultant for Eisenstein's film. Yet Podvoisky later admitted that he 'could not remember how [he] crossed the barricades'.[14] This is scarcely surprising, since he had not done so. Furthermore, Eisenstein himself was not present in Petrograd in either October 1917 or November 1920, although he would have read newspaper reports of both the Revolution and its more spectacular re-enactment and may well have seen the newsreel reportage of the latter. Even the design sketches for the production would have provided visual references for his cinematic re-enactment seven years later.

. . . .

Like *Potemkin*, *October* began as a larger-scale project also covering the Red Army's victories in the Civil War that followed the October Revolution. The film that eventually emerged was but a single episode from the original project, the scale of which can be seen from a report published in the film industry newspaper *Kino* on 6 November 1926, almost exactly a year before the actual tenth-anniversary celebration: 'Eisenstein and Tisse are to begin work on 1 January [1927] on filming an anniversary film on the grand scale. The film will be nine months in production and will include: the preparations for October; October at the centre [Petrograd] and elsewhere; and scenes from the Civil War.'

In fact it was Eisenstein and Grigori Alexandrov who began work on *October* in January 1927: as cameraman, Eduard Tisse's contribution was to come later. Eisenstein dictated the script to Alexandrov, who then read back his notes, which the two then discussed and revised. While the Committee considered the first version of the script, Eisenstein was cutting his film about collectivisation, *The General Line* (1929). At the Committee's insistence *October* was honed down to focus on the nine months from February to October 1917. The rest was to be covered by a second film that would be made if the time were available.[15] The censor's office Glavrepertkom also made changes so that, when Eisenstein was asked by an American correspondent who was writing the script, he immediately replied 'the Party'.[16]

On 8 March 1927 the script was finally accepted by the censors and five days later Eisenstein and his crew left for Leningrad, as Petrograd had become after Lenin's death early in 1924. Before he left Moscow, Esfir Shub, who had given Eisenstein his first cinematic experience re-editing imported films for Soviet distribution, showed him the documentary footage that she had found of the events of 1917 for her compilation film, *The Great Way* (1927), also commissioned for the tenth anniversary. Once in Leningrad, Eisenstein visited the historical locations – the Palace, the Peter and Paul Fortress and the Smolny Institute – with two of the men who had directed the events: Nikolai Podvoisky, already mentioned, and Vladimir Antonov-Ovseyenko, the man who had arrested the Provisional Government in the Winter Palace, both of whom are portrayed in the film.[17]

On 31 March Eduard Tisse returned from Berlin with a new Bell & Howell camera and the latest lenses. He was severely critical of the Sovkino studio's lack of interest in equipping the crew for a considerable amount of filming at night and in winter when the light that far north was less than adequate: 'It is typical that this trip was not only arranged on our own initiative, but quite independently and without any assistance from the organisation responsible. For Sovkino apparently the technical perfection of our production is quite beside the point.'[18]

The *Potemkin* triumvirate – Eisenstein, Alexandrov and Tisse – thus reassembled, shooting began with the scenes of fraternisation at the front. The scale of the film – undoubtedly *the* film of the anniversary year as far as the authorities were concerned – was gigantic. When Eisenstein had been handed the commission, Podvoisky had promised him, 'Leningrad Bolsheviks will provide the authors of *The Battleship Potemkin* with everything they need.'[19] The budget was originally estimated at 500,000 roubles but grew closer to 800,000, 20 times the budget for the average Soviet film at that time.[20] Eisenstein cut reviews of Cecil B. DeMille's *The Ten Commandments* (1923) out of German film magazines (since, for obvious reasons, the film was not released in the Soviet Union) and stuck them in his diary. *October* was meant to be the Soviet equivalent of *The Ten Commandments*, with Lenin substituting for Jesus Christ.[21] In a foretaste of the way that favoured directors were to be treated by Stalin in the 1930s (a decade in which Eisenstein was most certainly *not* favoured), he was paid more than any other Soviet film director – 550 roubles a month plus the same amount in extras – effectively twice as much as the other star name, Vsevolod Pudovkin, then filming *The End of St Petersburg*.

At least, though, the Sovkino studio was able to economise on sets and actors. Eisenstein was allowed to film inside the Winter Palace and the other buildings closely associated with the events of 1917. No sets had to be built. The leading Formalist writer and critic, Viktor Shklovsky, remarked, 'The Revolution has taken into its care museums and palaces that it does not know what to do with. Eisenstein's film is the first rational use of the Winter Palace. He has destroyed it.'[22] Pudovkin was filming in Leningrad at the same time as Eisenstein, who later recalled an elderly porter at the Winter Palace, who was sweeping up the glass from the 200 windows broken during the filming, remarking dryly, 'Your people were much more careful the first time they took the Palace.'[23]

Just as Evreinov had involved the population of the city in the 1920 re-enactment, so Eisenstein advertised in the Leningrad papers for the 50–60,000 extras he was seeking for the mass scenes. He claimed that 'Our search for "types" turned the city into a branch of the labour exchange. Our assistants grabbed people who looked right for the part and demanded their unquestioning obedience.'[24] The May Day parade through the city was filmed and used for the July demonstration in the film: the demonstrators were apparently surprised to find themselves carrying banners proclaiming the slogans of ten years before! Alexandrov later claimed that he had been arrested by the police as a counter-Revolutionary, and only released through the direct intervention of the newly appointed Leningrad Party chief, Sergei Kirov.[25]

14   Eisenstein and his crew

On 13 June the crew began the ten-day shoot of the storming of the Winter Palace. Because the filming took place at night the chief fire officer insisted on the installation of special safety fuses for the powerful lights but the electrical stores were all closed. It was the police who came to the rescue:

> The head of the Leningrad police, realising what it would mean to interrupt the filming, suggested that we went on a 'crime spree'. He, an electrician and I slid headlong down the arch of the General Staff HQ, threw ourselves into a car and rushed off to the biggest electrical store in Leningrad. The chief of police 'arrested' the guard. The electrician and I broke the locks and appropriated a couple of hundred of those ill-fated fuses. We put together a report on the deed and returned triumphantly to the Winter Palace.[26]

City officials had to work at night as extras and the Red Army was called in to help with the organisation of the crowds. As in 1920, when the safety fuses had been fitted and the lights switched on, the power supply to parts of the city had to be switched off, and for this Eisenstein's team again needed Kirov's specific permission. On 7 August the scene of the Palace Bridge being raised was filmed and on 20 August Lenin's arrival at the Finland Station. At the end of that month all the city's immigrants from the Caucasus were called up to play the Cossack soldiers in Kornilov's Savage Division: they controlled the city's shoeshining business and so there were no shoeshine boys on the streets for several days.[27] On 12 September the filming in Leningrad was completed and the crew moved to Moscow, where the statue of Alexander III that opens the film was being reconstructed. The final shots were completed on 11 October. Eisenstein had 49,000 metres of film to reduce to 2,000 by mid-October so that multiple prints of the film could be made for distribution in time for the anniversary on 7 November. He fell ill with exhaustion and was ordered to rest in a darkened room to restore his damaged eyesight.[28]

Grigori Alexandrov later claimed that Stalin himself had visited the cutting room at 4 o'clock on the morning of 7 November:

> Greeting us as if we had met before, he asked, 'Does Trotsky appear in your film?' 'Yes', Sergei Mikhailovich replied. 'Show me those parts.'

Stalin, severe, thoughtful, disinclined to chat, entered the room without a word.

There was no projectionist. I went into the booth myself and showed the reels depicting Trotsky. Eisenstein sat next to Stalin. After the screening Stalin told us about the demonstration by the Trotskyite opposition, which had turned into an open struggle against Soviet power, against the Bolshevik Party and the dictatorship of the proletariat, and concluded, 'Now you cannot show a film with Trotsky in it.' We managed to cut out three scenes with Trotsky in them. But there were two reels in which it would have been difficult to get rid of Trotsky by using the editing scissors, so we simply left them on one side and re-edited them in the course of November and December.

It was in fact only fragments of our film that were shown that evening in the Bolshoi Theatre.[29]

When his health recovered, Eisenstein continued to edit the film. He asked for 45 days extra to complete the projected first part, 'Peace to the Cottages', and another 15 for the second part, 'War on the Palaces' – both parts taking their titles from the Communist Manifesto. His request was refused and he was told to produce the completed film in one part, although he was allowed to do some extra filming. Given his earlier doubts about how some of the filmed material had turned out, the editing process was crucial and Alexandrov later estimated that the final version of *October* contained 3,300 shots, compared with 1,280 in *Potemkin* and 300–400 in the average Soviet film at that time.[30]

In an article published in December 1927 Eisenstein argued: 'The purely editorial work to be done on *October* is extremely difficult, demanding a great deal of time – for we are confronted with a whole series of quite complicated and unprecedented approaches to the various sequences and themes.'[31] On 14 January 1928 he showed the film to a small group of friends, including Alfred H. Barr, later director of the New York Museum of Modern Art, who noted in his diary, 'At times the tempo was too fast. The film seemed however a magnificent accomplishment.'[32] On 23 January Eisenstein wrote in his diary at lunchtime, 'I turned thirty today and *October* is one year old. At 9 p.m. I am showing the film to the government, the Central Committee and the Central Control Commission. *Va banque*. It's all or nothing.'[33] This hurdle overcome, the film was given a general release 'at a hundred theatres simultaneously'[34] on 14 March 1928. The publicity campaign set *October* against E. A. Dupont's *Variety* (1925). But it was another German film, *Love like Lightning* (1925),[35] starring Ossi Oswalda, the 'German Mary Pickford', that kept audiences away from Eisenstein's film, just as Allan Dwan's *Robin Hood* (1922), starring Douglas Fairbanks, had lured them away from *The Battleship Potemkin* the previous year.

Many of Eisenstein's admirers at home and abroad had in fact expected *October* to be a second *Potemkin* and their disappointment goes some way towards explaining the complexity of the film's reception. The director himself was appalled at the comparison and on 16 December 1928 wrote to the French critic Léon Moussinac: 'The greatest stupidity (found in almost all the German papers) would be to compare *October* to *Potemkin*. *October* is

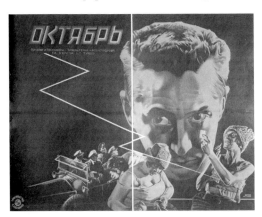

Soviet posters advertising
October, 1927

the dialectical denial of *Pot[emkin]*! And the main interest of *Oct[ober]* is in the bits and pieces that *bear no resemblance* to the "Battleship".'[36]

It had been Moussinac who, when comparing Eisenstein's film-making style with Pudovkin's, had tellingly remarked: 'An Eisenstein film resembles a shout, a Pudovkin film evokes a song ... Pudovkin incorporates in his films more study, more science, more intellectual effort than Eisenstein. He relies on method rather than inspiration.'[37]

. . . .

Eisenstein's version of the events leading up to the October Revolution of 1917 begins with a dedication 'to the Petrograd proletariat, heroes of the October Revolution'. There follows immediately another title telling us that the film has been officially commissioned by the Anniversary Committee chaired by Nikolai Podvoisky. After the credits the film originally began with a quotation from Trotsky, but that had to be removed after Stalin's visit to the cutting room. Instead, we have a quotation from Lenin, the leader of the Bolshevik Party and driving force behind both the October Revolution and the early years of Soviet power until his death in January 1924: 'We have the right to be proud that to us fell the good fortune of beginning the building of the Soviet State and, by doing so, opening a new chapter in the history of the world.'

Reel space, 1927

The first image is of a crowned head and this introduces the opening sequence of the film, showing the toppling of the statue of Alexander III, father of Nicholas II the last tsar, who was the one actually deposed in February 1917. Alexander III had ruled Russia from 1881 to 1894 after his relatively liberal father, Alexander II, who had emancipated the serfs in 1861, was assassinated in March 1881 by revolutionary terrorists in St Petersburg on the site where the Church of the Holy Blood now stands as a memorial. The period of repression that set in after the assassination very much identifies Alexander III with the depths of reaction and the weighty machinery of tsarist oppression which is conveyed by his ponderous statue. In his hands he holds the traditional symbols of power, the orb and sceptre, and both the sceptre and the pedestal are adorned with the double-headed eagle of the Russian Empire. In the terminology coined by Eisenstein these details are the 'attractions' from which the montage is constructed and from which it derives its meaning for both the film-maker and his potential audience.

Eisenstein shows us these symbols in close-up and, while to us the meaning of this sequence may be abundantly clear, a Soviet peasant – or even an urban worker – in the 1920s would have found the symbolism inaccessible, if not actually incomprehensible. To make matters even more complicated, the statue shown is not the real one, which had in fact only been unveiled in 1912 in the presence of Nicholas II and his wife Alexandra. The imagery of the statue in *October* may well have been influenced by newsreel footage of that unveiling. Some shots of the covering sheet as it falls away might well have given Eisenstein the idea for this deconstruction sequence.[38]

One of those campaigning for the statue's removal after the Revolution – and this underlines its symbolic significance – was the revolutionary poet, Vladimir Mayakovsky. In a poem entitled 'It's too early to rejoice', written in December 1918, which began 'We are seeking the future', he went on:

> Sow death in the enemy camp.
> Don't give in: take capital on.
> And does Tsar Alexander still stand
> On Uprising Square?
> Dynamite him![39]

Since the Bolshevik government eventually took Mayakovsky's advice, Eisenstein had to use a model made of *papier mâché*. The relative ease with which the model is deconstructed symbolises the relative ease with which the tsarist autocracy was itself toppled. With Eisenstein, however, things are rarely that simple and his symbolism is often tied up with the re-working of his own personal preoccupations. In his memoirs *Beyond the Stars* he discusses the effects of rain and the hollowness of statues such as the Statue of Liberty in New York but, more particularly, the maidens decorating one of his architect father's more extravagantly designed buildings in Riga, where Eisenstein was born and brought up:

Eisenstein's father's architectural maidens

It was probably my memory of them that led to my dismembering the giant statue of Alexander III with such mouthwatering excitement, in the opening episode of *October*. I doubt if I would have seized on the drama of the toppling statue, captured on film, but for the memories of Papa's maidens, somewhere at the back of my mind. And, if I add that the dismembered and overturned, hollow figure of the tsar served as an image for the overthrow of tsarism in February, then it is clear that the start to the film, recalling the defeat of Papa's creation using the image of the tsar himself, was about my own personal liberation from Papa's authority.[40]

In fact, although he would not have wished to admit it, Eisenstein is here using a technique advocated by his rival, the documentary film-maker Dziga Vertov who, in his 1923 manifesto *The Cine-Eyes: A Revolution*, had argued, in a section headed 'Montage in Time and Space', that the strength of cinema lay in its ability to create a new reality from fragments that in real life were unconnected or geographically separate:

> *The film camera drags the eyes of the audience* from the hands to the feet, from the feet to the eyes and so on in the most profitable order and it organises the details into a regular montage exercise … You are walking down a street in Chicago now, in 1923, but I force you to bow to the late Comrade Volodarsky, who is walking along a street in Petrograd in 1918 and who responds to you with a bow.[41]

The statue of Alexander III that is deconstructed here once stood in Moscow in the square in front of the Cathedral of Christ the Saviour, which was in turn originally erected to commemorate the victory over Napoleon in 1812.[42] A 1917 Russian guidebook to Moscow remarks: 'The monument to Alexander III is the work of the architect Prof. Pomerantsev and the sculptor Opekushin … Too colossal and ponderous, it is distinguished by the exceptional quantity and wealth of material used in its construction. The point of the monument is the grandeur and power of autocracy.'[43]

While a Moscow audience might well have appreciated the significance of these details and in particular understood the symbolic association between Church and State, the rest of Eisenstein's film takes place almost entirely in Petrograd and the positioning of the deconstruction of this statue at the beginning of the film might suggest to the uninitiated that it is actually taking place in Petrograd. Cinematic reality here takes over from actual geographical reality, as in Vertov's project, through montage. Nevertheless there are some fleeting shots that would probably have been universally understood, such as those where the Cathedral is clearly visible behind and above the statue, representing in Eisenstein's montage treatment the role of the Russian Orthodox Church as the power behind the imperial throne.

However, most of this would have had to be explained to contemporary mass audiences who would otherwise have been completely baffled. Many of them apparently still were. At the Party Conference on Cinema, which followed the film's première in March 1928, Alexander Krinitsky, head of the Party Agitprop Department, remarked, 'I think that *October* will be quite a difficult film for workers and peasants. In what conditions will *October* do well? Only if the Komsomol [Communist Youth League] launches a campaign round the film, organising explanatory work that will help the mass audience to "rise" to an understanding of this film.'[44] As it was, the process of explanation, which was attempted with this and other 'difficult' films, inevitably distanced spectator from film and destroyed much of its vivid immediacy. If a film could not be 'read' directly and immediately it was not fulfilling Lenin's 1920 maxim that 'of all the arts, for us cinema is the most important'.[45] It was for this type of relative obscurantism, for the 'intellectual cinema' in which he so fervently believed at this time, that Eisenstein was repeatedly criticised.[46] *October* was emphatically not a film that was 'intelligible to the millions', as the prevailing slogan of the time demanded.[47]

We are shown the inscription explaining whom the statue commemorates and then the double-headed eagle, the emblem of Imperial Russia, adorning the pedestal. Workers rush up towards the statue, mirroring the Odessa Steps sequence in *Potemkin*. Perhaps this is one small part of the 'dialectical negation' of *Potemkin* that Eisenstein mentioned to Moussinac: in the earlier film the workers had been mown down by the tsar's Cossacks (moving in a solid phalanx mainly downwards across the screen from left to right), whereas this time they will, ultimately, gain their revenge (moving more loosely in this opening sequence upwards from right to left). They erect a ladder against the statue's head and climb up it: the *papier mâché* was tough enough to support their weight. Again they move from bottom right to top left. A woman urges the others on and ties a rope around the tsar's left leg. His head and torso are similarly entwined. The autocracy is doomed and helpless, trapped by the tide of history.

According to Bolshevik ideology, the events of 1917 were a revolution of 'workers, soldiers *and* peasants', so the film then cuts first to soldiers cheering and waving their rifles in the air and then to a host of scythes wielded by invisible peasants. This visually-led transfer of ideas – first the 'montage of attractions', later 'intellectual montage' – was also the kind of montage technique that contemporary audiences had to be inducted into.

The first post-credit title appears: 'February. The proletariat's first victory on the road to socialism'. Almost certainly most contemporary audiences watching this film, however limited their knowledge of current affairs, would have known at least the rudiments of the history of 1917 and for them the word 'February' acts as a *warning* and the title thus creates a certain degree of ambiguity and suspense. They did after all know that February 1917 soon turned out to be less revolutionary than anticipated. It is however presented in the film as a *victory* because that is how it seemed to many at the time. The statue is toppled hesitantly and in parts: first the head, then the orb and sceptre, next the arms and legs. For a brief but telling moment the tsar is left exposed on his throne until the throne itself is toppled.

Because the original statue was not removed until 1921, rather than February 1917, there is here what Vertov called a montage of both time and space, creating a new and revolutionary version of reality: what appears in the film to take place in Petrograd in 1917 actually occurred in less dramatic form in Moscow four years later. The symbolic overthrow of tsarism is celebrated by a repetition of the shots of waving rifles and scythes, this time in reverse order. In this way the February Revolution is framed visually, and therefore also ideologically, by the activities of the workers, soldiers and peasants.

Implicitly, the workers', soldiers' and peasants' Revolution is accomplished, the autocracy overthrown. But the contemporary audience would have known otherwise so that it comes as no surprise when Eisenstein's warning is made explicit. The February Revolution is greeted by the bourgeoisie and the officer class and blessed by the Church. This is once again demonstrated by the use of detailed images juxtaposed through montage to provide a symbolic association of ideas.

(But those ideas have been confused by the translation of the titles. In Russian the next title is 'For all!' and this enables Eisenstein to question in the titles that immediately follow precisely what 'All' means. In the translation the appeal of the *February* Revolution is 'To the citizens of Russia!' – which, as we shall see, was the title of the Bolsheviks' appeal in *October* – and the force of the subsequent questioning is lost.) February is, it soon transpires, essentially a *bourgeois* Revolution, even though it was brought about by the toiling masses. February is therefore but a prelude to the *real* Revolution, that of the October of the film's title, and the aptly named Provisional Government is, as we shall shortly see, more provisional than even it had anticipated.

. . . .

From the Revolution the masses expect land, peace and bread – fundamental human demands that date back to the Old Testament and beyond, and that constituted an important part of the Bolshevik appeal to the working masses in both town and country in 1917. The soldiers at the front abandon their rifles, sticking their bayonets into the snow-covered ground and clambering out of their trenches in order to fraternise with the 'enemy'. They talk and pour one another beer, addressing one another as 'brother' and 'friend'. We see an Asiatic 'Russian' soldier trying on a German spiked helmet, while a German soldier tries on his fur cap. A German officer looks on and laughs: he is played by Eisenstein's cameraman for *October* and most of his other films, Eduard Tisse, in his only screen appearance. This brief fraternisation scene

Cameraman Eduard Tisse as a German officer

underlines the solidarity of the international working class, and simultaneously undermines the concept of patriotism in an imperialist war, where that class is mere cannon fodder in the hands of international capitalism. A Bolshevik agitator, using military headgear from both sides to illustrate his argument, explains this to a group of soldiers from the opposing armies.

Then, suddenly, the tsarist double-headed eagle – from the pedestal of the statue but shot from the opposite angle – intrudes: the threat to the Revolution is now both immediate and direct. Filmed from above to diminish his stature even further, a lackey crosses a tiled floor in the Winter Palace, bows low and proffers a silver platter with the government's note, passed to him in turn by two other lackeys: 'The Provisional Government will continue to honour the commitments made to the Allied powers.' In this, as in all the other explicit and implicit shots of the Provisional Government, there is a sense of a confined group of isolated men imprisoned by the trappings of the *ancien régime* and hermetically sealed *within* the old imperial Winter Palace *against* the realities of the new outside world. Their reality has surface but no substance.

To underline the shock of the change in fortunes, there is a violent shell burst. The shot of the imperial eagle is followed by the bayonets stuck into the ground. Artillery bombardment resumes and the soldiers return to their respective trenches. The war continues, the working class is betrayed. A heavy artillery piece is slowly lowered: at first this is intercut with shots of the front, showing the soldiers in their trenches. The workers and soldiers continue to be oppressed under the new régime as they were under the old. Then an intertitle announces: 'One pound of bread': in the cities bread-rationing is introduced. Now it is the women and children, queuing in freezing conditions for the bread promised by the Revolution but not yet delivered, who are the victims of war and class oppression. Eisenstein later complained: 'Both the territory and the time were against us. In its external appearance the city had already forgotten the "ten days that shook the world". Just as it was impossible to find a single starving and emaciated baby to film for the "bread queue", so we had to film many scenes to fit the routine of the Leningrad day.'[48]

In the background a sign advertises the sale of horse meat – scarcely a delicacy in the Russian culinary tradition! As the ration is gradually reduced, Eisenstein repeats the metaphor: we see the artillery piece being lowered as if to squeeze the working class, be they soldiers at

The queue for bread

the front, or women and children on the home front. In a further twist to the equation it is workers also who are forced by their circumstances to lower the artillery piece that here symbolises the oppression.

A series of intertitles describing the declining bread ration makes the growing pressure explicit: 'One pound of bread ... One half pound ... One quarter pound... One eighth pound.' Just after this last intertitle there is a fleeting shot in which an empty vodka bottle is barely visible in the bottom lefthand corner of the screen. The working class is reduced to drinking vodka to stave off the pangs of hunger for the staple diet of bread. This brief shot is significant because the production and sale of vodka, as of salt, was a tsarist monopoly at the time, so that the association with the old order is immediately obvious to a contemporary audience. Finally their situation becomes intolerable, they are desperate, and this elegiac sequence ends with the intertitle: 'The same old story — hunger and war.' There is no peace, no bread, no hope of land. Suspense is however created by the next title: 'But ...'

. . . .

For the working masses February has been a revolution of betrayed ideals. Their situation is dire – but at this very lowest point, when all hope of a better life seems lost, a saviour is at hand. Although Eisenstein would almost certainly have hated to admit it, he is here using techniques of pathos very similar to those of the many Hollywood directors in whose potboilers the virginal heroine was tied to the railway track by the villain, only to be snatched free by the hero as the train – apparently inexorably – approached. In *October* the heroine-mass, tied to the apparently inexorable course of history at the hands of a villainous bourgeoisie hell-bent on 'stopping the clock' at capitalism, is about to be rescued at the very last minute by the hero Lenin who will lead the oppressed to liberation in the Promised Land of the October Revolution.

The scene switches to the Finland Station in Petrograd, where Lenin arrives on 3 April 1917 from his exile in Zurich, having crossed Germany in a sealed train with the approval of the German authorities, anxious to undermine their Russian enemy and shorten the war by fomenting revolutionary activity. Serried ranks of workers wait in disciplined order. Their outward calm belies their inner turmoil. Searchlights from above move across the mass, slowly at first, then more frenetically: the crowd is restive and expectant. Eisenstein was disappointed with the takes for this scene: 'The "arrival" is terrible: only 3–4 metres of the long shots are usable and the rest is such a dog's breakfast – the lighting is all over the place and what's more it's all out of focus.'[49] This was one of several sequences that would have to be rescued on the editing table. The tension reaches its climax with the heroic, liberating arrival of their saviour, whom they greet with wild cheers: 'It's him! ... Ulyanov! ... LENIN!'[50] Banners proclaim allegiance to the Soviets and the Third International. There is a storm of enthusiasm and, in one of the most famous sequences from *October*, Lenin climbs on to an armoured car and speaks, his head moving against the background of the fluttering banner of the Petrograd Soviet.[51] Searchlights continue to range almost randomly across the crowd and this helps to increase the sense of urgency and tension. Lenin praises the workers and soldiers who have overthrown the monarchy, denounces the Provisional Government and promises the socialist Revolution, 'Socialist, not bourgeois'. Like a traditional religious saviour, he offers the masses hope in their hour of utmost trial. The main points iterated in the film summarise Lenin's so-called 'April Theses', which were published in the Party paper *Pravda* a few days later.[52]

Contrary to widespread belief, Eisenstein's *October* was *not* the first film to portray Lenin: that honour fell to the British film *The Land of Mystery*.[53] When it was released in 1920, Leonid Krasin, then Soviet plenipotentiary in London, acquired a copy and took it back to Moscow, where he showed it to a group of People's Commissars, including Lenin and his wife, Nadezhda Krupskaya.[54] From then on various unsuccessful attempts had been made to offer an alternative, Soviet representation of Lenin on Soviet screens. Hence in 1927 the Anniversary Commission made it more or less compulsory for Eisenstein to include a portrayal of the leader of the Revolution. Indeed, according to Alexandrov, the commission to film *October* included a specific instruction to this end from President Kalinin: 'We are counting on seeing in the film the image of Vladimir Ilyich, the Leader of the Socialist Revolution, the founder of the Soviet State.'[55]

Nonetheless, despite – or perhaps because of – this elaborate heroicisation, Lenin does not appear in *October* as an individual but as an embodiment of the elemental power of the mass, of the collective will. We need to remember that the tradition of secular portraiture in Russia had developed rather later than elsewhere in Europe because of the continuing insistence of the Orthodox Church, since the reign of Peter the Great itself effectively a department of state, that only saints and similar 'religiously correct' figures such as tsars could be represented in painted portraits. The reverse side of this coin was that the actual process of such representation, which before the Revolution was largely *still*, often imbued the subject with an aura of saintliness. The Bolsheviks had used this to their own advantage in newsreels in the early post-Revolutionary years so that audiences who had often never seen a *moving* image before assumed, for instance, that Lenin was either the new tsar or God's representative on earth, while in later years Stalin was not averse to deploying a variety of techniques derived from Christianity to suggest and reinforce his own quasi-divine status.[56]

There were inevitably risks for Eisenstein in including a representation of Lenin in his film, even though he had been specifically instructed to do so. It is in fact difficult to see how he could have portrayed the events of 1917, at least from the official Bolshevik point of view, without doing so. Following Lenin's death in January 1924, Stalin was quick to draw on the sense of collective grief to ground his own claims to be Lenin's true heir and to lay the foundations for his own personality cult. *October* was expected to play its part in the developing hagiography of the dead leader, now safely embalmed and publicly exhibited like one of the holy relics of the Christian tradition.

However, instead of using a trained actor, Eisenstein chose an unknown worker, Vasili Nikandrov, to play the part. Knowing that he was looking for a Lenin look-alike, the actor-director Vladimir Barsky, who had played Captain Golikov in *Potemkin* and was now filming in the Urals, sent Eisenstein some photographs of his 'discovery'. Nikandrov came to Moscow in March 1927 for screen tests and, according to Alexandrov, both Lenin's widow and his sister Maria gave their approval.[57] Nikandrov studied Lenin's writings, spoke to people who had known him and, as Alexandrov put it, 'grew' into the role. He was considered so convincing in some quarters that he later played Lenin on the stage of Moscow's Maly Theatre.[58] Eisenstein was, in principle if not always in practice, averse to the use of professional actors, at least as far as his silent films were concerned, feeling that greater realism was to be achieved by using ordinary workers and peasants, who represented certain 'types' – hence the recruitment advertisements that appeared in the Leningrad press. In the case of Lenin, having the part played by a worker – and Nikandrov had apparently once worked at the famous Putilov plant, which had played a significant part in the revolutionary events of 1905 – had the additional advantage that it emphasised the revolutionary's role as representative of the mass. Nevertheless, for Eisenstein, who had already applied this notion of 'typage' to the casting for both *The Strike* (1925) and *Potemkin*, the overriding factor about Nikandrov was that he *looked like* Lenin.

Despite this surface verisimilitude, Eisenstein was severely criticised by many of his contemporaries. Vladimir Mayakovsky, who was working on a poem on the anniversary theme at the time, attacked what he regarded as the superficiality of the characterisation: 'It is revolting to see someone striking poses and making movements like those of Lenin, when behind this exterior you can feel complete emptiness, the complete absence of life.'[59] Even before the film had been edited Mayakovsky had been among those highly critical of the idea of portraying Lenin at all. In a public debate on 15 October he said, 'Our Sovkino [studio] in the person of Eisenstein is going to show us a counterfeit Lenin, some Nikanorov or Nikandrov ... I promise that at the most solemn moment, wherever it might be, I shall whistle and throw rotten eggs at this counterfeit Lenin. This is an outrage [*bezobrazie*].'[60] In the circumstances it is hardly surprising that Eisenstein told Alexandrov: 'don't let anyone have a photograph of Nikandrov, and especially where he and I appear together ... And don't let anybody see them.'[61] Other contemporary Soviet critics also had their doubts about the portrayal: 'Lenin has turned out badly. The audience is faced with a rather brisk and fidgety little man. Ilyich's characteristic dash and liveliness have given way to an improbable fussiness. Antonov-Ovseyenko grows into the gigantic figure of the leader of the whole uprising.'[62]

For Antonov-Ovseyenko, or for anyone else other than Lenin to become 'the gigantic figure of the leader of the whole uprising' was, of course, neither historically nor politically correct. In Eisenstein's film this outcome was clearly accidental, but it was perhaps inevitable that, if Lenin were to be portrayed in this symbolic and impersonal way, he would fail to come alive for audiences as a human being and remain 'a rather brisk and fidgety little man'. His function is rather as a leading symbol in a film full of symbols. Indeed Nadezhda Krupskaya, who, let us not forget, had also seen *The Land of Mystery* in 1920, conceded that, if the film had a fault, it lay in the director's use of symbolism that would not in fact be 'intelligible to the millions':

> In the film *October* there is a great deal of symbolism. There is some symbolism that is accessible and intelligible to the mass: the toppling throne, the idols from St Basil's, etc. These symbols are very good: they help the viewer to make sense of the film, they provoke him to thought. But in the film there is much symbolism that will be little understood by the masses, and this is particularly true of the symbolism embodied in the statues – all the Napoleons and so on. The following symbol is probably also unintelligible: a sea of scythes that appears before the toppling of the thrones. To someone who had not seen pictures and sculptures that symbolise the mass peasant movement by scythes this image would probably be unintelligible and it would pass right over him.[63]

This was to become a familiar criticism of Eisenstein's film. Krupskaya was really agreeing with the implied criticism of other reviewers that Eisenstein was, in effect, producing a pedant's film for a peasant audience.

The critic Viktor Shklovsky, however, took a different view:

> After viewing some Eisenstein sequences a man who is intelligent and conversant with cinema said to me, 'That is very good. I like that a lot but what will the masses say? What will the people we are working for say?'

What can you say to that? ...

The times give Eisenstein an obligation to many and perhaps to all. The times have demanded their own cinema. Just as the industrialised elements of production appear in cinema to be at the same time artistically progressive elements, so the political task now plays one of the principal roles in cinema.

But we must not now produce works to gain applause, to please immediately and to please everyone.

We must give the audience time to mature to perception.[64]

As we shall see, the symbolism in *October* continues throughout the film.

. . . .

While the portrayal of Lenin failed to enthuse the critics, the screen Lenin certainly enthuses his screen audience. The last title summarising Lenin's speech emphasises that the Revolution must be 'Socialist, not bourgeois' but also tells us that after 'Five months of bourgeois government ... No Peace ... No Bread ... No Land.' The 'five months' here is rather confusing because it is through this title alone that the action of the film jumps forward now rather suddenly from Lenin's return in April to July 1917, known as 'the July days' and characterised here as the 'Days of the people's wrath'. Workers and soldiers are seen streaming across the Palace Bridge over the River Neva bearing placards and banners calling for: 'All power to the Soviets! ... Down with the Provisional Government!' (In fact, as we have seen, these shots show the 1927 May Day demonstration: only the slogans have been backdated to make the sequences look like authentic newsreel footage.) The workers' banners adorn the viewpoint at the eastern end of Vasiliev Island and the northern end of the Palace Bridge called Strelka (literally 'arrow'), which appears several times during the film. Outside the Bolshevik headquarters Antonov-Ovseyenko calls on the workers to remain calm and resist provocations from the authorities. His audience includes a group of armed sailors from the Kronstadt training base in the mouth of the River Neva just outside Petrograd. They are destined to play a key role in the coming uprising. But, for now, he tells them that an uprising would be premature: 'The Party will lead you when the time comes.'

Demonstrating workers converge on the junction between

Sadovaya Street (and not, as the English title says, Square) and the city's main artery, Nevsky Prospect, where the editorial offices of the reactionary evening paper, *Vechernyaya vremya* (Evening Times) are situated. In the background we can see the colonnade surrounding the Gostiny Dvor department store. The peaceful demonstration is intercut with shots of the barrel of a machine-gun. A confrontation is approaching but, when it comes, it is swift and brutal. Then a rapid montage of shots of the gun barrel taken from different angles provides a visual equivalent to the sound of a volley of gunshots. This first montage sequence consists almost entirely of three alternating shots: the gun pointing downwards to the left; the gun pointing upwards to the left, rather like the ship's guns in *Potemkin* (an erection?); a dark shot of the machine-gunner's face. In 'The Dramaturgy of Film Form' (1929), Eisenstein cited this sequence as a classic example of what he called 'logical montage':

> Montage: repetition of a machine-gun firing by cross-cutting the relevant details of the firing.
> *Combination a*):
> Brightly lit machine-gun. Dark one.
> Different shot. Double burst:
> Graphic burst and light burst.
> *Combination b*):
> *Machine*-gun.
> *Close*-up of the machine-gunner.
> *Effect almost of double exposure with rattling montage effect.*
> *Length of the pieces* – two frames.[65]

The 'rattling montage effect' constitutes Eisenstein's method of producing sound through image in a silent film. The workers disperse in panic. Some fall to the ground. There is a second sequence of visual machine-gunning, this time using slightly different shots of both gun and gunner. The gunner is smiling, almost laughing, as if he is literally achieving an orgasm through the pursuit of violence. The crowd drains out of the street. The crowd shots in this scene may be familiar to those who have never seen *October*, because they are the first of several sequences from the film that have subsequently been used as documentary film material. Because there are no individual characters in

Machine-gunning the crowd: emotional authenticity and 'logical montage'

this episode, and therefore no close-ups, the footage has been relatively easy to pass off as 'documentary'.

In an attempt to save one of the banners, a young worker finds his way to the banks of the Neva, where he disturbs a tsarist officer canoodling with his girlfriend under a parasol on the embankment steps at the Strelka viewpoint. The worker is wearing the horizontally striped undershirt characteristic of the Russian Navy, which suggests that he may be a Kronstadt sailor in civilian disguise. But for the bourgeoisie the key issue is that he is a Bolshevik, and therefore a mortal class enemy. Bourgeois vengeance is swift. As his girlfriend's parasol moves left to right, the officer notices the worker and identifies him as a Bolshevik. In parallel movements the girl swings the parasol through the air as the

Working man meets bourgeois woman

worker moves his banner away. While the girl looks on disdainfully, the officer floors the worker while, in the foreground, another parasol announces the arrival of a monstrous regiment of bourgeois ladies intent on a manhunt. Their faces contorted with rage, contempt and hatred, they join in the fray, one of them even tearing the Bolshevik banner with her teeth.

The scene cuts to the Palace Bridge, the crowd fleeing north to the workers' districts from Nevsky Prospect as the machine-gun fires once more. In the foreground an empty carriage comes to a stop on the bridge as the white horse pulling it falls to the ground. Here, as in *Potemkin*, white represents purity and innocence. The horse's legs, as it struggles to stand again, are intercut with the legs of the bourgeois lady as she stamps on the banner's pole. She is in effect performing a dance of death. The pole breaks, while on the bridge the horse falls finally to the ground. But the worker is still fighting to resist the officer, so the ladies tear his striped undershirt and shirt off his chest, exposing a target for the tips of their parasols, which they then plunge into him in another vicious orgy of violence. An elderly bourgeois gentleman looks on, laughs and applauds. And all this is done with gloves on! Eisenstein wanted to re-create a tableau he had seen in 1906 at the age of eight in the Musée Grévin (the waxworks) in Paris, and in a book in his father's library, which illustrated the vengeful fury of bourgeois Parisians towards the activists of the 1870–1 Paris Commune.[66]

The revenge of the bourgeois ladies

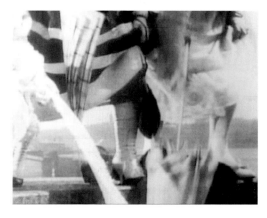

The director later argued that the sequence was also influenced by Emile Zola's *Germinal* and displayed the same faults as that novel:

> Our film *October* suffered in a similar way in the sequence dealing with the events of July 1917. At all costs we wanted the historical incident of the worker Bolshevik who was beaten and murdered by the brutalised bourgeoisie to be imbued with the 'tone' of the Paris Commune. The result was the scene with the ladies hitting the worker with their parasols: the scene is quite different in spirit from the general mood of the period before October.[67]

Raising the bridges

There is an echo here of the bourgeois women on the Odessa Steps in *Potemkin* but there they were fellow victims of tsarist oppression: in *October* they are opposed to the workers and represent the *February* as opposed to the coming *October* Revolution. Eisenstein appears to be saying here that *Potemkin* provided a more accurate and authentic portrayal of the pre-Revolutionary role of the bourgeoisie than did *October*. Nevertheless, the hatred that these women feel is quite tangible, as is the precise nature of their 'allegiance' to the Revolution. Their stabbing motions pierce the audience's psyche as well as the body of the worker, who here represents one instance of Eisenstein's notion of synecdoche, of *pars pro toto*, of representing the whole by its part. Here the body of a single worker symbolises the oppression of his class as a whole by the bourgeoisie.

The horse is now lying dead across the bridge, as is a young woman in a white blouse, her long hair stretched out across the middle divide where the bridge is raised, normally to allow shipping to pass underneath. In what David Bordwell has described as 'an epically extended moment' their deaths and what happens to them on the bridge

symbolise the martyrdom of the working class.[68] The power of the imagery at this point has been compared to the role of the stone lions in *Potemkin*.[69] We then see a man who, it later transpires, is a minister in the Provisional Government speaking on the telephone. He gives the order to raise the bridges to cut off the workers' quarters from the centre of the city. The young woman's body slides back down the bridge, as the sphinx at Strelka looks impassively on. The corpse of the murdered worker lies on the steps, water lapping over it. This segues into the next scene, where the bourgeois ladies, fresh from the kill, watch some bourgeois men throwing copies of the Bolshevik paper *Pravda* into the Neva, and then join in. They are joined by a nun, emphasising once again the reactionary role of the Church, and a woman we shall later recognise as a soldier in the Women's Battalion of Death. To complete the bridge episode, the horse is finally separated from its carriage and drops into the Neva. Symbolically the proletariat and the bourgeoisie are now irrevocably separated one from another. The banners of the demonstrators are also seen floating down the river: the Revolution is literally being washed away.[70]

The First Machine-Gun Corps is marched in disgrace through the streets, surrounded by cavalry and 'disarmed for solidarity'. Bourgeois onlookers, including the elderly gentleman we have seen before, denounce them as 'turncoats' and 'traitors', appellations that Eisenstein plays with in later titles. The soldiers are led past the Bolshevik Party headquarters, which have been ransacked. The Revolution would seem to be in ruins.

. . . .

There is a contrast between the chaos of the ransacked headquarters and the undisturbed order of the Winter Palace. Kerensky strides along a corridor and climbs the Jordan Staircase.[71] This is the first sequence in *October* in which Eisenstein 'plays' with the objects within the Palace. Alexandrov recalled that the tsar's apartments had been 'preserved intact'.[72] Eisenstein was overwhelmed and his sense of wonder can be felt in many of the sequences filmed in the Palace interiors:

> Museums by night –
> especially museums of sculpture –
> are amazing!

> I will never forget my nocturnal walk through the halls of ancient sculpture in the Hermitage, during the 'White Nights'.

> I was then filming scenes for *October* in the Winter Palace; I walked along the passageways connecting the Winter Place to the Hermitage just as the light was shifting.

> It was a fantastic spectacle.

The milky bluish twilight streamed in through the windows facing the embankment.

And the white shadows, cast by white bodies of Greek statues, seemed to come alive and float in the blue gloom.[73]

In this dream-world Kerensky is in fact strutting up the same flight of stairs over and over again, and this was intended as an ironic visual comment on an endless search for power that takes Kerensky nowhere because his ascent is interspersed with titles proclaiming his different positions, suggesting that he is something of a one-man band, who represents nobody but himself. Eisenstein cited this sequence as a classic example of 'intellectual montage', as 'the case in which the same conflict tension serves to achieve new concepts, new points of view, in other words, serves purely intellectual ends'.[74] He went on:

Kerensky's rise to (untrammelled) power and dictatorship after July 1917. Comic effect is achieved by *intercutting titles denoting ever higher rank* ('Dictator', 'Generalissimo', 'Minister of the Navy and

Kerensky's symbolic rise through the trappings of power.

the Army', etc.) with five or six sequences of the staircase in the Winter Palace with Kerensky ascending the *same* flight each time.

Here the conflict between the kitsch of the ascending staircase and Kerensky treading the same ground produces an intellectual resultant: the satirical degradation of these titles in relation to Kerensky's nonentity.

Here we have a counterpoint between a verbally expressed, conventional idea and a pictorial representation of an individual who is unequal to that idea.

The incongruity between these two produces a purely *intellectual* resolution at the expense of this individual. Intellectual dynamisation.[75]

Finally his character is introduced as: 'The hope of the Nation and the Revolution ... Alexander Kerensky'[76] and, both metaphorically and actually, he reaches the threshold of the tsarina's apartments. His figure is overshadowed by a statue which is holding a garland of flowers on high, apparently ready to 'crown' him, and he is attended by the tsar's footmen, or 'lackeys' as the intertitle styles them. We are shown his elaborate boots and gloves: in an echo of the hollow statue of Alexander III he is fascinated by the external trappings of power. The footmen comment ironically: 'A true democrat! ... A "ROYAL" democrat!'[77] By contrast with Lenin, Kerensky is a dilettante, 'playing' at revolution and democracy, alone and isolated from the mass. Whereas Lenin has been shown in an active and decisive posture in the 'real' world, Kerensky vacillates in the fairy-tale world of the Winter Palace. He is more 'feminine' than the bourgeois ladies as he stands at the threshold of the *tsarina's* apartments.

At this point Eisenstein introduces another of his 'intellectual' metaphors. A mechanical golden peacock (its face resembling that of one of the tsar's lackeys), a gift from Tsar Nicholas II to his wife Alexandra, preens itself, spreads its tail and turns its back on the camera. Kerensky hesitates again but, as the peacock turns its back, he enters the royal apartments. The doors open twice and, as he enters, we see his back, as we have just seen the peacock's. According to Yuri Tsivian's analysis of this sequence, 'Eisenstein was hoping to achieve the effect of Kerensky entering the peacock's arsehole.'[78] By penetrating the peacock at its moment of

The statue and the
peacock

display, Kerensky is penetrating the essence of the excessive and empty display of the world of Nicholas and Alexandra. As the doors close behind his entourage, so the peacock returns to its original position. A close-up of a lock confirms that he is imprisoned in a world of private fantasy.

By way of contrast *October* now switches to the prison cells where the Bolshevik 'turncoats' and 'traitors' are incarcerated. Sailors, soldiers, workers and peasants are all clearly represented. We are told by the next title that on 6 July, as part of the crackdown on revolutionary opposition, the Provisional Government ordered Lenin's arrest. Once again the prospects for the Revolution seem bleak. A brief and tranquil interlude shows us Lenin's thatched hideout in the misty marshes near Razliv on the Gulf of Finland. An intertitle claims that it was from here that Lenin directed the Sixth Party Congress, which planned an armed uprising, but historians now believe that the Bolshevik leadership at this time was characterised by weakness and confusion, that Lenin's hold was tenuous and that the Party had in fact *missed* its opportunity for armed insurrection.[79]

There could be no greater visual contrast between the simplicity and tranquillity of Lenin's hideout and the magnificence of the Winter Palace. Back in Petrograd Kerensky broods, first in the tsarina's apartments and then in the tsar's. Eisenstein uses the caption 'Alexander Kerensky ... in the chambers of Empress Alexandra'. The Russian original translates more accurately as 'In the apartments of Alexandra Fyodorovna ... Alexander Fyodorovich'. By playing on the fact that Kerensky's first name and patronymic share the same root as those of the last tsarina, Eisenstein is able to imply a continuity and a close resemblance. The intimacy of this resemblance is underlined by the sight of *Kerensky's* clothes strewn across *her* bed. The next titles ask: 'In the chambers of Alexander III' ... 'Is he to be Alexander IV?' But the

The reality of Lenin's hideaway

The unreality of Kerensky's
power

continuity goes beyond the implication of a shared imperial heritage for, in showing Kerensky in the *tsarina's* bedroom, surrounded by all *her* finery, Eisenstein is also able to suggest a degree of 'unmanly' weakness and indecisiveness both on the part of the Prime Minister and the Provisional Government. His one clear act, taken hesitantly in Nicholas II's personal library, which is heavily furnished in what passed for the 'English' style – masculine in the sense of a gentleman's club – and where he is framed by huge ivory tusks, is a reactionary one, the reintroduction of the death penalty.[80]

This action leads into the scene criticised by Krupskaya. Kerensky climbs a Victorian Gothic staircase, folds his arms and surveys the scene. Below him is an ornate grand piano with a telephone placed on top of it. Kerensky's pose is echoed by a statuette of Napoleon, his arms also folded. To an audience that knows its history the inference is clear: Kerensky is a second Napoleon and, like his implicit mentor, he will usurp and betray the ideals of the Revolution. His intentions are symbolically clarified as he plays with a set of decanters, moving them into different positions and finally bringing them into place, fixing them together with a stopper that is shaped like a crown. Kerensky, like Napoleon, wishes to be Emperor. Crystal glasses and decanters emblazoned with the imperial emblem, and rows of model soldiers, complete the analogy. But Kerensky is not alone in his ambitions. As the stopper is screwed tight on to the decanter set, a factory siren wails its warning: 'The Revolution is in danger!'

. . . .

General Kornilov is approaching Petrograd and the city's workers abandon their factories, shipyards and plants to defend the city. Kornilov had been appointed Commander in Chief of the Russian Army by Kerensky on 18 July and he had been the architect of the reintroduction of the death penalty for desertion and a number of other reform proposals over which Kerensky had vacillated. On 26 August Kornilov demanded that Kerensky hand power to him as military dictator, a demand that, not surprisingly, was refused.[81] Kornilov is advancing 'In the name of God and Country', for religion and for patriotism. The phenomenon of religious values is universalised by Eisenstein through a sequence of religious images from the familiar shapes of the Russian Orthodox Cathedral of St Basil in Moscow, through the Catholic Baroque, a Muslim mosque and a laughing Buddha – symbolising the great religions of the world – back to primitive tribal masks. Eisenstein later quoted this sequence as a paradigmatic example of intellectual montage:

> Here we have an attempt to use the representation [of gods] for anti-religious ends. A number of images of the divine were shown in succession. From a magnificent Baroque Christ to an Eskimo idol.[82]

> Here a conflict arises between the concept 'God' and its symbolisation. Whereas idea and image are completely synonymous in the first Baroque image, they grow further apart with each subsequent image. We retain the description 'God' and

show idols that in no way correspond with our own image of this concept. From this we are to draw anti-religious conclusions as to what the divine as such really is.

Similarly there is here an attempt to draw a purely intellectual conclusion as a result of the conflict between a preconception and its *gradual tendentious discrediting by degrees* through pure illustration.

The gradual succession continues in a process of comparing each new image with its common designation and *unleashes a process that, in terms of its form, is identical to a process of logical deduction*. Everything here is already intellectually conceived, not just in terms of the resolution but also of the method of expressing ideas.

The conventional *descriptive* form of the film becomes a kind of reasoning (as a formal possibility).

Whereas the conventional film directs and develops the *emotions*, here we have a hint of the possibility of likewise developing and directing the entire *thought process*.[83]

This is a first step towards the 'intellectual cinema' that Eisenstein was to explore in subsequent writings. The idea was perhaps more clearly explained in Eisenstein's 1930 speech at the Sorbonne in Paris:

It is a matter of producing a series of images that is composed in such a way that it provokes an affective movement which in turn triggers a series of ideas. From image to emotion, from emotion to thesis. In proceeding in this way there is obviously a risk of becoming symbolic: but you must not forget that cinema is the only concrete art that is at the same time dynamic and can release the operations of the thought process. The thought process cannot be stimulated in the same way by the other arts, which are static and can only provoke a thought response without really developing it. I think that this task of intellectual stimulation can be accomplished through cinema. This will also be the historic artistic achievement of our time because we are suffering from a terrible dualism between thought (pure philosophical speculation) and feeling (emotion).[84]

The appeal to religion in its diversity of forms is, for the director, universal but essentially dishonest, just like the appeal of patriotism in its diversity of forms. Both religion and patriotism are, in Marxist terminology, opiates of the people, both fallacious, and essentially reactionary focal points for popular allegiance: only the Bolsheviks represent the *true* demands and needs of the mass for bread, peace and land. The appeal to patriotism is represented by a montage of shots of epaulettes and military decorations, the worthless baubles of a patriotism that has exploited the workers. Through a similar visual intellectual montage the two appeals – religion and patriotism – are merged.

The statue of Alexander III magically reassembles through a montage of reverse-action footage, and the depth of the Revolution's betrayal has been reached. In a question-and-answer session with his students some 20 years later Eisenstein recalled that, in the Meisel score, this reassembling of the statue was accompanied by the opening music for the film being played backwards: 'First a statue was taken to pieces. Then it flew back together again. The music for the film had been written, and the orchestral score was completed. It was also done backwards: that is, there was music for the statue being taken apart, and the same musical phrases were played backwards as it flew back together.'[85]

The restoration of the values of the old order is in turn blessed by a repetition of some of the religious images just seen, now smiling their approval, and, more directly, by the priest whom we saw blessing the February Revolution in the opening sequence where the statue was deconstructed. The priest's reappearance makes him the Orthodox equivalent of the vicar of Bray and emphasises the ambiguities of the February Revolution.

Kornilov sits astride a white horse. In this instance the colour white represents a claim to virtue rather than virtue itself. He is shot from below to underline ironically the pomposity of his pretensions. This shot fades into another statue of Napoleon, this time echoing Kornilov's horseback pose. The analogy is not pure fantasy: there is some evidence that, while in prison, Kornilov had read about the life of Napoleon and come to the conclusion that he was destined to play a similar role in the history of Russia, hence the white horse.[86] Kornilov and Kerensky are both compared to two different statuettes of Napoleon, one as man of action

(Kornilov), one as man of inaction or thought (Kerensky): both are traitors and counter-revolutionaries, both megalomaniacs, lusting illicitly for power. They are 'Two Napoleons'. Which of the two will win through? The one, Kerensky, lies motionless and helpless face downwards on a couch, not knowing what to do: he has the trappings of power but not the power itself. His statuette of Napoleon crashes to the ground and smashes: his ambitions are symbolically destroyed. He uses cushions to drown out the sound of the factory sirens, which represent the workers, the only hope for the defence of Petrograd and thus the only guarantors of the Revolution. The other, Kornilov, advances on the capital, armed with (British) tanks and armoured cars, supported by the

Kornilov

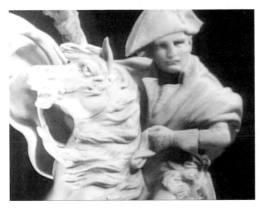

Kerensky

The two Napoleons

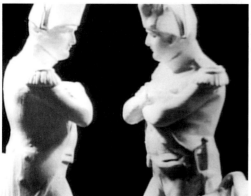

Savage Division of Cossacks who ironically, given the Cossacks' reputation as horsemen, arrive by train.[87]

. . . .

The Provisional Government, in the hands of the ineffectual Kerensky, is powerless to defend the city and this task is left to the city Soviet. Workers advance across the screen, their banners fluttering in the darkness. The angled shots emphasise the 'uphill' nature of the struggle, but the title assures us that 'Kornilov shall not pass'. The crowd, led by a sailor, break into the prisons and liberate their imprisoned comrades. The so-called 'turncoats' and 'traitors', the Bolsheviks, are armed to defend the Revolution. The ironic repetition of these titles reminds the viewer that it is those who hold constitutional power, rather than the Bolsheviks, who are the real turncoats and traitors.

For the first time we see the Bolshevik headquarters at the Smolny Institute (which ironically was formerly a finishing school for young ladies). Outside we see workers streaming towards the building: one of the approaching vehicles is an armoured car with two drum-like turrets, which we are to see several times again in the course of the film. Inside the building we see the caches of revolvers and rifles and the organisation of bundles of pamphlets ready for distribution. Arms are being distributed to the proletariat. The darkness enhances the sense of anticipation.

Elsewhere another group of 'turncoats' and 'traitors' are altering the railway points and curtailing the advance of Kornilov's Cossacks so that they can be visited by a Bolshevik delegation intent on persuading them to change sides. There is an anxious moment of apparent confrontation as the Savage Division unsheathe their swords: a close-up shows us that these are inscribed with the motto 'God is with us'. Eisenstein lavishes attention on expressive close-ups of their faces in a way that presages facial images from his later films, such as *Alexander Nevsky* (1938) and *Ivan the Terrible* (1944–6). The Bolshevik agitators arrive, one of them a sailor from the *Amur*. Although this is the name of a river in the Far East dividing Siberia from China, and may in the context of Petrograd be seen as symbolising the size and complexity of Russia, Eisenstein, with his extensive knowledge of languages, would have been aware of the play on words with the French word '*amour*' or love, and would in any case have known that *Amur* is the Russian name for Cupid and that in its plural form (*amury*) it means 'love affairs'. The sailor thus brings the idea of fraternal love to the Savage Division.[88]

The two Bolsheviks address the 'enemy' and explain the message of their leaflet, which 'spoke their language' offering bread, peace and land. The Cossacks sheathe their swords again, dance the *lezginka* and fraternise. Eisenstein later commented on this sequence:

> With an abrupt, rhythmic drawing, when the music is really hammering it out, you can cut sections according to the rhythm of the music. They will coincide. In the film *October* there is the *lezginka* episode. The 'Savage Division' is approaching Petrograd. They are met by workers' organisations, and they fraternise. The Petrograd lot do a Russian dance and the 'Savage Division' respond with a *lezginka*. Two rhythms meet. There the accumulation of montage was driven by the rhythm of the *lezginka*. There was a precise coincidence. But it could have been done quite differently. You could cut a section for each musical accent, and add a new section with each beat. Or you could have a long section of conversation, accompanied by this chopped-up rhythm.[89]

But, as Eisenstein noted, he chose to use the *lezginka* as the dominant rhythm here. In a veritable orgy of celebration the Bolsheviks join in: the Savage Division has changed sides. This sequence is intercut with a

The Savage Division: a Cossack converted

smiling wooden figure (like those in the sequence of the gods) nodding its approval and with shots of Kerensky, who continues to take refuge under the tsarina's cushions, as his power ebbs away. A title tells us that General Kornilov has been arrested, but it is clear that it was the Bolshevik-organised proletariat that created the necessary conditions for this and not the Provisional Government. Kornilov was in fact arrested on 1 September 1917 but for considerably more complex reasons than Eisenstein's film suggests.

. . . .

In a series of stills a rifle is assembled from its constituent parts: this echoes and reverses the reconstitution of the tsar's statue. Symbolically this sequence denotes the need for proletarian self-help: the mass must make the best of the available materials, it must literally forge its own weapons to defend the Revolution that the bourgeoisie have hijacked. The title reiterates this: 'PROLETARIAN, LEARN TO USE YOUR RIFLE!' Then: 'The Bolsheviks must seize power!' We see the serried ranks of the Petrograd Soviet training on a makeshift parade ground. Their disparate nature is illustrated by close-ups of their different footwear, yet another example of *pars pro toto* or synecdoche, where the variety of footwear reflects the variety of the participants. The next title reads: 'This will be the last and decisive battle!' (The more usual translation of this line from the 'Internationale' is 'And the last fight let us face!') The climax is approaching.

There is a montage of shots of mass meetings and debates. Antonov-Ovseyenko is among the speakers addressing the crowd. We now jump ahead again, this time to 10 October: the Bolshevik Party Central Committee is heatedly discussing the question of an armed uprising. The scene shifts to the smoke-filled room in which the Bolshevik leaders are deliberating. Trotsky argues for delay, while Lenin, with Stalin at his side,[90] nominates 25 October 1917 as the date for the seizure of power, a proposal that is unanimously accepted. The agreed date is then acclaimed by the mass waiting outside who raise their weapons in the already familiar gesture. The deadline for the victory of the Revolution has been established: progress can now be measured against that deadline and the suspense that leads to the climax of the film can therefore be created.

We cut to the headquarters of the Military Revolutionary

Committee charged with planning the uprising. Doors swing open and shut repeatedly and suddenly it is 24 October, the eve of what was to become known in the Soviet period as the Great October Socialist Revolution. The second half of Eisenstein's *October* is devoted to the detailed run-up to that event. Two Mensheviks conspire in a corridor.[91] Looking round shiftily, one of them momentarily appears to recognise a seated figure whose face is swathed in a scarf as if he were suffering from toothache. It is in fact Lenin in disguise. He has finally arrived at the Smolny Institute. We see concentric circles being drawn round the Winter Palace on a map of Petrograd: a title tells us that Lenin has taken over the direction of the armed uprising.

Armed struggle in itself is not enough. In their previous underground political activity the Bolsheviks had long since learned the significance of agitation and propaganda in the battle for the hearts and minds of the masses and we have already seen their methods applied successfully to the conversion of the Savage Division. They draft an appeal 'TO THE CITIZENS OF RUSSIA!' Eisenstein then shows us a copy of the original declaration: 'The Provisional Government has been deposed! State power has passed into the hands of the Petrograd Soviet of Workers' and Soldiers' Deputies.' It is 25 October 1917, 10 a.m. Presumably this is an indication of the Bolsheviks' confidence in victory: at 10 a.m. the *following* morning they will proclaim that victory. In the meantime, the workers stream *by night* from their districts towards Smolny. Where previously we saw packages of leaflets being passed around in the corridor, now we see weapons being trundled in. The entire building becomes a hive of activity. By contrast with Bolshevik activity, the Mensheviks stand idly and suspiciously by, looking effete and ineffectual, one of them partially concealed behind a sign announcing 'Class Mistress', playing on the dual meaning in Russian (and indeed in English) of the word 'class'.[92] A guard collects the identification papers of those arriving and stores them on the point of his bayonet, in a peaceful deployment of the weapons seen in the opening sequences of the film – not exactly turning swords into ploughshares, but almost!

The commissars order detachments to strategic buildings in the city such as the telegraph office and the telephone exchange. Some forces depart in armoured cars (including the one with the twin drum-turrets) and lorries, some on foot. Reinforcements gather, the tension

The Menshevik as 'class
mistress'

increases, heightened by the darkness and the smoke. A storm brews in
the sky – just as the storm-tossed waves that open *Potemkin* presaged
an impending upheaval in the old order. An image of the Smolny
Institute façade as dawn is breaking fades to the title: 'The morning of
October 25th.'

Dawn has now broken and Eisenstein cuts to shots of the cruiser
Aurora (Dawn), which has been ordered to sail up the River Neva to fire
the shot that provides the starting signal for the storming of the Winter
Palace. The bridges have been raised once more to cut the workers'
districts off from the city centre and this allows the cruiser to sail
unhindered on its mission. Once it is in position, however, the most
urgent priority is to reconnect the workers' districts with the centre. With
the *Aurora* in the background and factories in the distance, Bolshevik
sailors creep forward while government soldiers retreat. The sailors
capture the Nicholas Bridge and it swings sideways to the closed position.
Given the pathos that accompanied the raising of the bridges earlier in
October, their reconnection represents a moment of triumph, but one that
also reconnects the audience with the sacrifices made earlier for the
Revolutionary cause.

But the reconnection of the bridges does not reconnect the
proletariat with the bourgeoisie. On the contrary, the minister on the
telephone, whom we saw earlier, is beside himself.[93] The trams run again
and sailors from the *Amur* disembark with their arms near the Winter
Palace. Meanwhile, Kerensky is desperate. Leaning on the ornate grand
piano while announcing himself as 'Minister of War', he telephones the

stables of the Cossack Regiment. (Neither this regiment nor the Cossack battery defending the Winter Palace are the same as Kornilov's Savage Division: the Cossacks served in various units in the Russian armed forces at this time.) The call is answered by the stable lad, who is obviously a Bolshevik sympathiser, because he lies to Kerensky, telling him that the Cossacks are already saddling their horses, and then hanging up. While the Prime Minister waits in vain for the Cossacks to give him the military assistance he expects and now so desperately needs, their horses munch away undisturbed on their fodder, while the stable lad sits down again and draws on his pipe in a gesture of what the next title ironically calls 'Neutrality'.

Once again we see the text of the Bolshevik appeal to the citizens of Russia. Inside the Palace, Kerensky, retrieving his cap from the strings of the piano, and still surrounded by his faithful entourage of tsarist lackeys, somewhat half-heartedly resolves to drive to the front line in order to lead his loyal troops back to crush the Bolsheviks. But, once he is outside the isolating confines of the Winter Palace, even he realises that his power has evaporated. He begins a defiant speech to his remaining retinue but then collapses into the back-seat of the car and flees to Gatchina, one of the tsar's country estates outside Petrograd, in a Rolls-Royce flying the US flag. He escapes therefore from the city that is the cradle of the Revolution to an estate representing the *ancien régime* under the protection of a foreign flag.[94] Kerensky is thus a double traitor to both class and country. The earlier analogy with Napoleon is continued through the pose that he strikes in the car, and by his gestures. As this captain leaves his sinking ship, the gates of the Palace are closed once more against the realities of the outside world. The Provisional Government, or what remains of it, is now completely isolated and devoid of outside support. The final confrontation is drawing ever closer.

A detachment of loyal cadets marches under the caryatids of the Winter Palace to come to the rescue of the Government, but it is too late. Nevertheless an officer tries to boost their morale: his puny figure is contrasted with the overpowering caryatid behind him. The Palace itself is defended by a remarkable group of rather fearsome, masculine, or at least sexually ambiguous, women called the Women's Battalion of Death. Their 'masculinity' contrasts with Kerensky's 'femininity' displayed earlier in the film. Outside, the officer enjoins the loyal cadets

Kerensky's departure from
the Winter Palace

to fight the insurrectionists 'To the last drop of blood!' Inside, ranks of
men and women march in, while the statues gaze impassively on, some of
them adorned with abandoned coats or bottles.

The women soldiers strip to their underwear and sit on the tsar's
billiard table, making themselves up, a bra draped over the cue stand. One
older woman, a tsarist medal pinned to her breast, wraps a cloth round
her feet, which suggests that she is a peasant, but one suffering from the
false consciousness induced by military baubles. This allusion is both an
echo of a previous image and a foretaste of later discoveries.

Outside, in the Palace Square, the defending cadets are building
their barricades. Kerensky is still in flight. Eisenstein then introduces a

A 1917 postcard of the Women's Battalion

rather confusing cut to the opposing side, beginning with a close-up of a gun turret and showing both sailors and soldiers. A Cossack from the Savage Division passes a sailor from the Baltic Fleet (thus encompassing two geographical ends of Russia) a note summoning delegates to the crucial Second Congress of the Soviets and the sailor gives him directions. Inside the Smolny Institute, between a pile of apparently abandoned typewriters in the foreground and rows of chairs being moved in the background, we see the delegates registering their presence. The chairs are carried off and the scene switches to room 16, where the Menshevik delegation is meeting. They wear caps and spectacles or pince-nez so that they look like the 'eternal student' from a Chekhov play. The Socialist Revolutionaries, the main rivals to Lenin's Bolsheviks, are meeting in room 20. Other delegates come from

Eisenstein's version of the Women's Battalion

the front, from the East, from the Baltic Fleet's base at Kronstadt, from the Ukraine, from Siberia. The Siberian delegates seem overwhelmed at the size and splendour of the building. The point of this sequence of introductions is to emphasise that all strata and areas of the country are represented at this Congress: it is, in effect, the country in microcosm.

The sequence ends with a series of shots showing the chairs being set out inside the hall, the façade of the Smolny Institute at night – a shot we have seen before that re-establishes the tension of the wait for decisive action – followed by a dark silhouette of the women guarding the façade and roof of the Winter Palace. Inside the Palace we see the guards on every floor and landing. A row of glasses of undrunk tea introduces the title: 'The Provisional Government had lost power but continued to exist.' The leader's chair is empty: the Prime Minister, as we have already seen, has fled to Gatchina. This is a cue for another cut to Kerensky, concealing himself ever deeper in his overcoat as his Rolls-Royce carries him into exile. Back in the Palace the members of the Provisional Government are shown for the first time. They are clearly representatives of a particular class, gender, generation and social order. We are told that they too have drafted an appeal to the people of Russia, but it is 'correct' and legalistic and demonstrates a complete lack of understanding of the problems that concern the mass of the population, problems already identified by the Bolsheviks under the triple slogan – bread, land, peace.

. . . .

Eisenstein then takes us back to the Smolny Institute and the Second Congress of the Soviets. It is now the night of 25/26 October 1917. The Congress is opened by the Menshevik/SR Central Committee, which dominated the membership of the Congress. The opening speaker (a Menshevik we have seen before in the sequence where Lenin arrives disguised as a man with toothache) argues for delay and a constitutional handover of power, echoing the words of the Provisional Government's own appeal that it alone is the lawfully constituted government of Russia and thus associating the Mensheviks with the bourgeoisie as class enemies. The film then cuts to a room where the Military Revolutionary Committee is meeting simultaneously. An intertitle – making an elision between the Committee and the population at large, which suited Bolshevik ideology rather than historical accuracy – informs us: 'But the people decided otherwise.' *Actions* speak louder than *laws*. Petrograd, Russia's capital,[95] is already in the hands of Revolutionary workers, sailors and soldiers, and practical power of that kind is what counts.

A mark is pencilled on a map of the city to indicate the position that the cruiser *Aurora* has reached and the film then cuts to a shot of the ship at anchor in the Neva. Another mark on the map designates the Peter and Paul Fortress (on the opposite side of the Neva from the Winter Palace) as the site for a party of sailors to go ashore. The film cuts to this happening. A cross on the map shows the spot where a guard-post is then set up. Next an arrow is drawn past the Stock Exchange across the Strelka viewpoint and we see the armed encampment that has been set up near where the Bolshevik worker was murdered and *Pravda* cast into the river. Then the junction of Nevsky Prospect and Sadovaya Street is marked on the map and shown on screen, followed by the Moika River, which runs inland close to the Palace Square. Gradually the workers are taking back the city of Peter the Great, taking their own history symbolically into their own hands. Finally we come back to the Winter Palace, both on the map and on screen.

Inside the Palace the Provisional Government, minus its Prime Minister, awaits its fate. Outside in the Palace Square, everything is quiet. Back in Smolny the Military Revolutionary Committee, discussing the final assault on the Winter Palace, almost apologetically goes into secret session. In the hall, where the Congress of Soviets is meeting, the Menshevik is still speaking, accusing the Bolsheviks (rightly, as it transpires) of hatching a military plot against the lawful government. He predicts 'hunger and ruin instead of bread'. His assertion leads to uproar. As his predictions become more extreme – 'The country's ruin will be the Bolsheviks' destruction', 'But the Revolution will also perish!' – he is shouted down by a Bolshevik: 'Down with the lackeys of the bourgeoisie!' But the Menshevik is also chairing the meeting and the next item on the agenda is the election of the Presidium. He asks the delegates to approve the Menshevik/SR slate. Their supporters are 'Not so many'. Then the Bolshevik slate is put forward. Their support is overwhelming – we see the delegates waving their admission cards – and the defeated Mensheviks and Socialist Revolutionaries leave the platform.

A banner is unfurled on the platform proclaiming the Bolshevik slogan 'All power to the Soviets!' There is a burst of frenetic activity: doors open and shut, people crowd corridors and staircases, telephones are used – and the focus of attention passes to the Military Revolutionary Committee. More copies of the Bolshevik appeal 'To the Citizens of Russia' are collected for distribution. Outside we see the Revolutionaries swinging into action but, whereas in previous scenes, they have been moving *towards* the Smolny for instructions, now they are moving *away* from it to put their instructions into effect. They leave as they arrived: on foot, by lorry, and by that same armoured car with the twin drum-turrets.

The Winter Palace is encircled in 'a ring of steel': contemporary audiences might have picked up on the association between the Russian word for steel (*stal'*) and Stalin's name as 'man of steel', even though he was not involved in these events. Those guarding the Palace against Revolutionary attack are passed the Bolsheviks' ultimatum, written by Antonov-Ovseyenko, giving them 20 minutes to surrender to avoid bloodshed. A small boy clambers between the feet of one of the Bolshevik sailors, eager to witness this moment of history. The two Bolshevik delegates hand the ultimatum to a defending woman soldier: they joke between themselves about her gender and decide to evade the issue by addressing her as 'Hey, friend!' She reads the note disdainfully and takes it off to her superior officers. The two Bolsheviks wait for a reply: a series of shots of Petrograd establish that the whole city is also waiting. Some of these shots have been used before, establishing continuity of waiting, and some are new.

Inside the Palace, their glasses of tea now upturned and abandoned, the members of the Provisional Government are also waiting. As dawn breaks over the city – both the Peter and Paul Fortress and a factory are shown – the curtains in the Palace are lowered shutting reality out finally and completely. One elderly member of the Government symbolically strums the strings of a lyre carved on a glass panel. The timeless sculptures gaze down on the proceedings. Shots are exchanged and one carving has its nose blown off. In the unreal world of the Winter Palace, one of the women soldiers dreams of love rather than hatred, a dream inspired by the Rodin sculpture of 'Springtime' (*Le Printemps*), which shows a couple embracing. Her head droops in contemplation and the thoughts provoked by the notion of love lead some of the women defending the Palace to abandon their rifles and surrender. 'One by one, the soldiers of the Death Battalion surrendered.'

In contrast to the parasol-wielding bourgeois ladies attacking the lone worker at the Strelka viewpoint earlier, these women are redeemed because Bolshevism is returning their 'natural' feminine instincts of love and motherhood to them. But this represents the conservative Stalinist gender ideology of the late 1920s and beyond, rather than the Revolutionary ideals of gender equality and liberation that were current in 1917. In the Palace Square a street lamp goes out: the last hope for the *ancien régime* has been extinguished. The intertitle 'Time was running out' leads into a clock consisting of a mechanical owl, another ornamental clock from the tsar's collection.

If most of the women have now surrendered, the Cossack battery has still to be persuaded. Bolshevik agitators and sailors from the Baltic Fleet enter the Palace through the cellars where many of the treasures of the Hermitage Museum are stored. They find themselves in the Department of Egyptian and Assyrian Antiquities. We are told that there are 1,100 rooms in the Palace and they do not know their way around. They ascend the Gothic wooden staircase where, earlier in the film, Kerensky had struck up a Napoleonic pose. As in that earlier shot, we see the grand piano with the ill-fated telephone on top of it. They pass the kitchens, which miraculously are still functioning undisturbed. They enter the state apartments. Meanwhile other agitators are at work in the main courtyard trying to win over the Cossack battery. An officer arrives unexpectedly and abuses a soldier for leaving his post. The English translation has: 'You dirty ... How dare you leave your post!' This not only reverses the Russian order, it bowdlerises it. In the original Russian, the insult is the worst possible term of abuse and would most accurately translate as the American term 'motherfucker'. In Russian the insult also comes *after* the reprimand and leads with a certain intellectual logic into the shot of a statue of a mother and child, entitled *The First Steps*. The gentleness of this sculpted portrayal contrasts sharply with the harshness of the officer's insult and reinforces – retrospectively from 1927 – the conservative notion that Bolshevism will make the world safe for 'normal' motherhood. With a similar intellectual logic, the scene then switches back to the inside of the Palace itself, where a woman officer is training some of her remaining troops, their relationship an ironic parallel to the motherhood role traditionally ascribed to women in European culture. The others sit around talking, exercising, waiting. There is a whiff of decadence about their behaviour. For Eisenstein, busy repressing his own homosexual inclinations at this time, the Provisional Government has placed these women without men in an 'unnatural' position.

The minister we have seen earlier trying to get through on the telephone to have the bridges over the Neva raised is now addressing the cadets defending the Palace. He tells them the Bolsheviks have presented the Provisional Government with an ultimatum. He has their half-hearted attention until he says: 'We shall not surrender Russia to the Bolshevik–German spies!' The association of the Bolsheviks with the German enemy had been a refrain of anti-Bolshevik propaganda, fuelled by Lenin's return in April 1917 in the sealed train from Zurich with the approval of the German authorities, and reiterated by Kornilov during his attempted coup in August. But in October 1917 the cadets have had enough: after this remark the speaker is almost universally ignored as they contemptuously go on reading, eating or generally fidgeting. Bolshevik sailors from the Baltic Fleet are already overhead on the roof. There is a brief shot of them looking down which reminds the observant viewer of the shots of the workers' quarters in *The Strike*. Outside in the courtyard the Cossacks have been persuaded to surrender. Their guns are covered but, as we shall shortly discover, they remain trapped in the Palace compound.

The film switches back to the Congress. This to-ing and fro-ing between Winter Palace and Smolny Institute is Eisenstein's way of representing visually the dual power by which Russia was governed in 1917 and the gradual transfer of real power from the one to the other. The hall is now filled with smoke after several hours of discussion. Another Menshevik is speaking. Wearing army officer's uniform and clearly unaware of what has been going on outside on the streets, he asks how the Bolsheviks propose to seize power. To this challenge he also adds provocation: 'The Army's not with you', then: 'The frontline troops ... are not with you!' The wounded veterans in the audience are puzzled, then incensed. Banging their crutches on the floor, they shout him down. One wounded soldier is so angry that he mounts the rostrum to speak. Others carry a banner declaring the Twelfth Army's support for the Soviets. This is reinforced by shots of soldiers in the field raising their rifles to demonstrate their support: in contrast to the officer, these soldiers rally to represent their constituency. Like the Provisional Government, the officer class has lost the constituency – and above all the power, authority and influence – that it once had. The hall breaks into enthusiastic applause as war front and home front are brought together by a montage of alternating images.

Then a soldier breaks into the hall to announce that the Cycle Battalion has come over to the Bolsheviks as well. The next montage sequence mixes shots of his face with rotating cycle wheels and clapping hands. The wheels are reminiscent of a sequence in Fernand Léger's film *Le Ballet mécanique* (The Mechanical Ballet, France, 1924), an experimental short exploring the relationship between rhythm and motion, a film that Eisenstein would certainly have seen and noted on his

Eisensteinian metaphors

travels. To an audience nowadays the notion of a cycle battalion playing any significant role in battle might seem faintly ludicrous, but they would have had a speed and flexibility that no other troops could have matched at that time, and been especially effective in a city like Petrograd. In contrast to the harp-playing hands, Eisenstein regarded this example of 'emotional dynamisation', the 'emergence of a concept, of a sensation from the juxtaposition of two disparate events' as a success: 'The pathos of the adherence of the Cycle Battalion to the Second Congress of Soviets is dynamised by the fact that, when their delegates enter, abstractly spinning cycle wheels (association with the battalion) were intercut. These resolved the pathetic content of the event as such into a perceptible dynamic.'[96]

In the Winter Palace the sailors on the roof drop a grenade through an opening on to the defending troops below. In the ensuing chaos the gates to the Palace, topped by the double-headed eagle, the insignia of the tsars, are opened, allowing the Cossack artillery to abandon their positions, surrender finally and change sides, crossing the Palace Square to join the Revolutionaries under the famous archway, which was built to join the two wings of the General Staff Headquarters and to commemorate Russia's victory over Napoleon. That this change of allegiance happens in the shadow of the military HQ gives it added pathos, but only, of course, for an audience that is aware of this! The Palace gates are padlocked behind them, leaving the Provisional Government even more imprisoned and isolated than it was before. The ministers appear to be asleep, and have certainly still not replied to the ultimatum. 'NO REPLY'. Their images presage some of the darker visual characterisations to come in *Ivan the Terrible* and, to a lesser extent, in *Alexander Nevsky*.

The Congress of the Soviets drags on, largely because the Mensheviks continue to insist that there must be no danger of bloodshed. The title tells us that they 'Discoursed': 'Intoned' would have been a better translation of the Russian '*peli*'. Eisenstein comments on their behaviour through the ironic use of images drawn from the Smolny building itself: an angel holds his hands in prayer, three harpists 'harp on the same old tune' causing an elderly soldier to try to clean his ear out with his finger and then cover it up with his cap. Eisenstein later described the analogy as a mistake, a failed attempt at 'emotional dynamisation': 'The mellifluous peace overtures of the Mensheviks at the Second Congress of the Soviets (during the storming of the Winter Palace) are intercut with harp-playing hands. A purely literary parallelism that does nothing to enliven the material.'[97]

The film cuts to a shot of the angel on top of the Alexander Column in the centre of Palace Square, erected as a monument to Russia's victory over Napoleon: the statue is seen from several angles looking down on the proceedings in the Winter Palace. We are reminded of the continuing period of waiting by a series of static shots of the city and the various 'actors' in the drama that is unfolding: sailors, soldiers, politicians. While the Bolsheviks, through their Military Revolutionary Committee, have already effectively organised the coup and the subsequent transfer of power, back at the Congress the Menshevik speaker drones on, now accusing the Bolsheviks of wanting to force the pace of historical events and denying their ability to deliver their promises. As he speaks, a Bolshevik delegate on the platform drums his fingers on a copy of the newspaper *Rabochii* (The Worker) proclaiming in a banner headline their slogan of land, peace and bread.

. . . .

At long last this Bolshevik takes the rostrum: 'The time for words has passed!' In the Palace Square the two delegates who had earlier delivered the Bolshevik ultimatum to the Provisional Government, and had since been waiting for the non-existent response, now remove their white flag and abandon their wait. The new speaker is greeted with the stamping of varied footwear (military boots, civilian shoes, peasant felt boots or *valenki*), representing the varied audience, and enthusiastic applause. As he speaks, the Revolutionary forces open fire on the Winter Palace.

In a series of images that, in the absence of any newsreel footage of these crucial historical events, have acquired the status of documentary authenticity, all the various strands in the Revolutionary movement come together into the liberating, carnival-like climax of 'The Storming of the Winter Palace'. As Yuri Tsivian has pointed out, there are, in fact, a couple of brief shots in which the firing gun is so positioned as to give the impression that the caryatids supporting the Palace are themselves experiencing an orgasm.[98] The images of gunfire are interspersed in another montage sequence with different Bolshevik speakers at the Congress – a woman, a worker and a wounded soldier seen earlier – demanding 'We want peace!', 'We want bread!', 'We want

The caryatid's machine-gun orgasm

land!' These speeches are intercut with the tinkling of the chandeliers in the Winter Palace as the old order trembles. They conclude with the 'The signal'. A single shot fired from the *Aurora* symbolically causes the camera to iris in on the empty main corridor of the Winter Palace. A technique familiar from early silent films, including those of Charlie Chaplin as 'The Tramp', this denotes closure, in this instance the end of the *ancien régime*. In a ricocheting reaction, the ministers in the Provisional Government fall back into their seats. Eisenstein recalled in his memoirs:

> I remember filming in the Winter Palace one night in October 1927 (for the film *October*). In the Palace rooms I achieved a plastic re-creation of the impressions made by the *Aurora*'s guns. The echo rolled through the rooms and reached a room where everything had been covered by white sheeting and where members of the Provisional Government were awaiting the fateful moment – the establishment of Soviet power – wrapped up in fur coats.
>
> A system of 'iris' diaphragms, in a correctly gauged rhythm – an opening and shutting out of views of rooms – attempted to capture the echo's breathing rhythm as it resounded through the galleries. The crystal chandeliers tinkling in reply to the rattle of the machine-gun fire on the square was more successful and remained in the audience's memory.[99]

Outside on one of the city's bridges, which Eisenstein claimed 'parodied the idea of unity and solidarity', a small group of elderly citizens whose clothing makes them obvious Eisensteinian 'types', representing the defunct social order, constitute 'The Committee for the Salvation of the Country and the Revolution'. We have seen one of them before applauding the fatal stabbing of the Bolshevik worker by parasol near Strelka. As they cross the bridge, they are stopped by another Bolshevik sailor from the *Amur*. Their claim that they are trying to save the Provisional Government is ridiculed by a visual metaphor showing the abandoned coats and hats of the ministers, suggesting clearly that their government no longer has any substance to it. The aged, wizened mayor, representing the *ancien régime*, is contrasted with the young and muscular sailor. Their protestations are in vain. He holds up the palm of his hand to halt them in their tracks. In his memoirs Eisenstein recalled:

> It was half-way across that bridge that the huge figure of the sailor arose – he was cast in the same mould as those sailors who locked the Nicholas Bridge [shut] and was the Baltic equivalent of those sailors in the Black Sea fleet who sailed through the admiral's squadron in *Potemkin*. Simply by raising a powerful arm he scattered the procession of old men: the last bastion of the supporters of reaction ... ran away.[100]

The image of the sailor's upraised palm cuts to further cannon fire as the assault on the Palace continues unabated.

Just as the shot from the *Aurora* 'forced' the Provisional Government ministers to sit down, so this fusillade 'causes' the Congress delegates to stand in celebration. The Menshevik speaker returns to the platform and protests 'most emphatically', but Menshevik *words* have by now been overtaken by Bolshevik *action*. As the crowd storms through the archway into Palace Square, a large clock displays the time: it is midnight on 25/26 October 1917. The Revolution comes at the bewitching hour of midnight: it is an event too large in its implications to be confined within the limits of a single historic day. One of the defenders of the Palace is a cadet firing a machine-gun: this sequence has obvious echoes of the earlier machine-gun attack on the demonstrators at the intersection of Nevsky Prospect and Sadovaya Street. It thus reinforces the idea that the old order has not learned any lessons from the past. A Bolshevik soldier, bullets strung across his chest, falls wounded, face down into a puddle: he is to represent, *pars pro toto*, all the Revolutionary heroes who fell in the storming of the Winter Palace.

As thousands of armed attackers swarm across Palace Square, the remaining women soldiers defending it retreat from their barricades back inside the building. The wounded soldier rises from the ground, removes his cap and shouts encouragement to his comrades as they rush past him in hot pursuit. He falls back to the ground. The attackers take the women defenders by force, a foretaste of what they are about to do to the Palace itself: again this is illustrated *pars pro toto* by a single instance of person-to-person combat, the woman defender appearing between the attacking man's legs before she is pushed to the ground. The child seen earlier urges the attackers on. A sailor climbs the main gates through which both Kerensky and the Cossack battery have already fled the building. Symbolically he uses the emblem of the tsarist crown on the gates as a foothold as he scales them. As he clambers over the top, he throws a grenade down. Pistol in hand, he sits astride the gates, waving the

The mob storms the Winter Palace staircase

attackers 'Forward!' He throws another grenade and this blasts the gates open for the crowd to stream into the Palace.

We see the attackers rush along the main corridor that is familiar from earlier shots. A very young and frightened cadet fires at the crowd in self-defence. He and his fellows try to defend themselves with bayonets but are quickly overwhelmed. The crowd hastens up the staircase that we have associated with Kerensky's rise to power. There is a chase through the wine cellars. Bottles broken symbolise blood spilt. Cowering in the tsarina's bedroom, some women defenders search for a hiding place behind the bed hangings. The pursuing Bolsheviks discover the tsarina's commode and laugh mockingly. An explosion outside causes one woman to jump into another's embrace. Another two women creep forward right to left across the screen, their bayonets protruding like substitute phalluses: when they fire at the Bolsheviks, one of the first pair of women jolts in pain as if she has been anally raped. In a sense, though, it is the old régime, and indeed the Winter Palace itself, that is being raped in an orgy of Revolutionary fervour that raises disturbing questions about the pleasure of destruction.[101]

While the assault continues outside, one of the Bolshevik sailors (another from the crew of the *Amur*) uses his bayonet to pierce and penetrate the tsarina's eiderdown. This clearly acts as a sexual symbol because the woman sailor experiences another frisson, but this time one of pleasure rather than pain. He gazes at the icons and other religious symbols and the family portraits in the bedroom. As his eyes move down a nude statue of the Madonna to her genitalia, the films cuts to an image of a bedpan and then a bidet with a chamberpot beside it. He spits in disgust – either at the unwonted luxury or the association of ideas that, at least in Eisenstein's mind, probably lay behind it – and bangs the eiderdown so that there is an explosion of feathers in the air, paralleled by an explosion of activity both outside and inside the Palace.

Antonov-Ovseyenko leads a group of Revolutionaries to find Kerensky and his Government, unaware that the Prime Minister has already abandoned his post. While the attack continues frenetically, down in the cellars the looting is beginning. Men and women workers help themselves to bottles of wine. Meanwhile upstairs the defenders are surrendering their weapons. As they do so, they are frisked for what they in turn have looted from the building. One young soldier has taken a small portrait of Nicholas II; another has a cap full of spoons, which are confiscated and added to the pile of looted goods retrieved. Instead of being punished (or even shot) he is gently admonished, his cap ruffled in his face. This is Revolutionary mercy.

In the cellars Bolshevik sailors restore order: one sailor from the *Aurora* wields his gun to smash the bottles from the grasp of the looters and then the actual wine racks are smashed in an orgy of Revolutionary destruction, rather than an advertisement for teetotalism. This is Revolutionary justice. This time the liquid that flows across the screen is not the workers' blood but the tsar's wine. Osip Brik, apostle of the 'literature of fact', complained that this scene was not historically accurate:

> Any departure from historical truth is permissible only when it is taken as far as complete grotesque when the idea that it might in some way correspond to reality cannot even arise … Everyone knows that the battle for the wine cellars after the Revolution was one of the murkier episodes of October and that the sailors did not merely smash the cellars but tried to drink them up and refused to shoot the people who had come to take the wine … But when a real sailor efficiently smashes real bottles the result is not a symbol or a poster but a lie … [102]

Upstairs the boy we have seen earlier sits on the throne, stands beside it, lies on it in a series of jump cuts – all the time cheering the Revolution on.

Looting the wine cellars of the Palace

He represents the future that is now being born. Downstairs Antonov-Ovseyenko leads the crowd across the marbled floor, seen at the beginning of the film, when the footmen brought the announcement that the Provisional Government was to continue the war and betray the Revolutionary ideal of peace. Symbolically the ill done then is now being undone. The only troops now defending the Provisional Government are three frightened young cadets and Eisenstein concentrates on one who is cross-eyed, to emphasise his lack of clear vision. They are disarmed and the crowd surges forward to the room where the ministers are awaiting their fate. The minister who earlier had problems with his telephone connections urges his colleagues: 'Gentlemen. Let us meet them in a most dignified manner.' The ministers hurriedly take their seats and don their coats, as if appearances will have any significance at this historic moment. The crowd smashes its way into the room, surrounding the ministers. Antonov-Ovseyenko mounts the table and tells them they are all under arrest. They hand him what would appear to be their letters of appointment and, surrounded by sailors from the *Amur*, he announces 'On behalf of the Military Revolutionary Committee ... I declare the Provisional Government deposed!' We see his handwriting on a piece of paper on the table with the historic date 25 October 1917.

Eisenstein then cuts to a clockface labelled 'St Petersburg' with the precise time of the moment of the handover of power. A series of clockfaces then shows the time across Russia and the world to mark this moment of universal significance in the history of humanity. In St Petersburg it is 2.17 a.m. and in Moscow 2.36 a.m, and equivalent times in New York, Berlin, London and Paris are also shown in close-up. The camera sweeps upwards from bottom right to top left, echoing the movement of the crowd toppling the statue in the opening sequence. What that crowd began has now been completed. One shot reveals that this clock with multiple faces, like the preening peacock and the swivelling owl, comes from the tsar's collection.

From this we return to local detail. In the throne room the small boy has fallen asleep on the throne. The Revolution has been accomplished and he can sleep in peace: the future is now assured. A rotating montage of clockfaces – which, Eisenstein later argued, 'added a further graphic dimension to the fusion of all the different indications of time into an awareness of that single historic hour'[103] – merges into applause from the delegates to the Congress of Soviets, intercut with

Clocks mark the historic
hour of the October
Revolution

some representative close-ups. The delegates stand and, against the background of a banner proclaiming 'All power to the Soviets!', Lenin, as befits the superstar of the Revolution, finally appears to address the Congress. This is the first time we have seen him since he took charge of events. The applause even wakes the elderly soldier who had muffled out the speeches of the Mensheviks and gone to sleep. He joins in the clapping and cheering.

Lenin proclaims: 'Comrades! The Workers' and Peasants' Revolution, which the Bolsheviks have always deemed necessary, has been won!' Shots of tear-off calendar entries for Wednesday, 25 October 1917 and Thursday, 26 October 1917, with their equivalents in the Gregorian calendar, are shown to remind us yet again of the historic dates.[104] Lenin's tumultuous reception is intercut with shots of his handwritten text, and of the printed decrees on peace and land. Unlike the Provisional Government, the Bolsheviks have kept their promises to the people and the victory that had been thwarted in *The Strike* and *The Battleship Potemkin* is now finally achieved. Just as the released version of *October* began with a quotation from Lenin, so too it ends: 'We must now

Bolshevik promises kept: the decrees on peace and land

set about building a proletarian socialist state in Russia.' The final shot shows the façade of the Smolny Institute.

When Eisenstein's film was released ten years after the events that it depicted, he wrote:

> *October*, this film – a difficult commission difficult to achieve – which was intended to convey to the audience the mighty pathos of those days that shook the world, which set out our new approach to filmed objects and facts, which acted on its audience using new and difficult cinematic methods that required keen and sustained attention, is finished. Now the audience has its say![105]

. . . .

Writing nearly half a century after *October* was made, Grigori Alexandrov made an unfortunate claim. Among the film's achievements were:

> First its absolute and convincing veracity [*pravdivost'*], the documentary quality [*dokumental'nost'*] of its depiction of real historical events. It is no accident that in later years many shots from the film have been compared in terms of their authenticity to newsreels. They have become textbook images, 'quoted' as documents in other films and displayed in exhibitions devoted to the history of the Revolution.[106]

Alexandrov attributed these qualities of authenticity to the careful preparatory work that had gone into the film, to the collaboration of those such as Podvoisky, Antonov-Ovseyenko, Krupskaya and others who had actually participated in the original events depicted, to the use of the original settings like the Winter Palace and the streets of Petrograd instead of sets, to the enormous assistance afforded to the film-makers (in terms of access, staffing, power supplies, etc.) by the Leningrad authorities.[107]

The undeniable fact that 'in later years a whole number of shots from the film have been compared in terms of their authenticity to newsreels', does not, however, mean that they are 'authentic' in a way that a historian would understand the term when applying it to a document. The ambiguous status of these shots is rather a reflection on the careless idleness of subsequent film-makers, including many makers of documentary films for both cinema and television, who have not taken the trouble to verify their sources properly.[108]

The 'authenticity' of *October* has been called into question by many critics ever since the film was released. The first criticisms, as we have seen, were of the depiction of Lenin and of relatively minor details, such as Brik's objections to the portrayal of the sailors' behaviour in the wine cellars of the Winter Palace and his perceptive conclusion that 'Eisenstein does not want to think of cinema as a means of showing actual reality; he has pretensions to philosophical film treatises.'[109]

Later writers have pointed to the undoubted fact that Eisenstein's portrayal of the October Revolution is very much a Bolshevik one. It is difficult to see how it could have been otherwise in a Soviet film commissioned for the tenth anniversary celebrations. I have pointed out some of the historical inaccuracies en route through this examination of the film, beginning with the 'montage of time and space' that the deconstruction of the statue of Alexander III represents. There are many others. But, in my view, the question of historical authenticity is as much of a red herring for *October* as it is for *Potemkin*. Eisenstein was a film-maker and theorist, not a historian. Some years later, after his unproductive spell abroad in the United States and Mexico, he noted that 'The centre of gravity of my latest works (*October*, *The Old and the New* [1929, aka *The General Line*]) lies in the field of experimentation and research.'[110] In his Sorbonne speech in 1930 he had argued that in *October*:

> The street shooting was played entirely by volunteers: almost all of them had played a more serious game in 1917 than ten years later in 1927! This gives us the opportunity to re-create the atmosphere and the truth of events.[111]

The *re-creation* of the 'atmosphere and the truth of events' on screen is not necessarily anything like the same exercise as the historian's attempt to *explain* those events. As we have already seen for our discussion of the 1920 Evreinov reconstruction of 1917, the very act of re-creation deforms the original events themselves, as does the act of memory, whether individual or collective.[112] Whereas in *Potemkin* Eisenstein used pathos and tragedy to convey the ethos of the failed 'First Russian Revolution' of 1905, in *October* he uses the techniques of comedy, including parody, to communicate in particular his sense of the absurdity of various aspects of the *ancien régime*. He repeatedly parodies, though admittedly somewhat ambiguously, the grandeur and pretension of the Winter Palace, using repetition and reversal, satirising Kerensky's ascent of the staircase as an act of hollow and pointless ambition, poking fun at the Women's Battalion, playfully toying with a variety of objects – from the tsarina's bidet, through the icons, eggs and clocks, to the preening peacock. The Palace is another world, a lost world of crowns and crystal, contrasted with, and isolated from, the 'real' world outside, joining it only in the climax to the film.

Part of Eisenstein's polemic against Vertov's notion of documentary realism lay in the central issue of the way in which objects were represented (or 'recorded' as Vertov would have put it) on screen:

> The representation of an object in the actual (absolute) proportions proper to it is, of course, merely a tribute to orthodox formal logic, a subordination to the inviolable order of things.

> This returns periodically and unfailingly in periods when absolutism is in the ascendancy, replacing the expressiveness of antiquated disproportion with a regular 'ranking table' of officially designated harmony.

> Positivist realism is by no means the correct form of perception. It is simply a function of a particular form of social structure, following on from an autocratic state that has propagated a state uniformity of thought.

> It is an ideological uniformity that makes its visual appearance in the ranks of the uniforms of the Life Guard regiments.[113]

The representation of the objects is therefore not 'objective' but ideologically and culturally *loaded*. It had been Eisenstein's intention, in both his stage and screen work during the 1920s, to try to use the montage of the associations carried by various objects (as, say, in the 'gods' sequence in *October*) to create an emotional – and by now also an intellectual – charge that would (pre-)determine how the audience would react to a particular given stimulus. In this sense, *October* represented a further stage in his attempts to realise that ideal. The attempts at 'intellectual montage' in *October* are a logical development from the earlier 'montage of attractions' in *The Strike* or the transitional montage in *Potemkin*. Eisenstein himself later remarked that '*October* was a swing in one direction – from concrete historical narrative to "generalised" abstraction and thence to the inevitable formal experimentation and over-refinement.'[114] To some extent he repeated these attempts in *The General Line*, released as *The Old and the New*, but in his later films he was experimenting in other ways – with the use of sound, music and colour, for instance.

. . . .

The 'formal experimentation' in *October* that Eisenstein later judged to be an 'over-refinement' was of greater concern to him as a film-maker than was any distortion of a historian's ideal of truth or authenticity. There is no reason why it should have been otherwise. Eisenstein was not, after all, and certainly never claimed to be, either a historian or a documentary film-maker. Instead, as far back as 1928, he argued: 'Now that we have discovered what constitutes a word, a form, a fragment of speech in cinema language, we can begin to pose the question of what we can *express cinematically* and how.'[115]

A contemporary editorial, summing up the critical reception for *October*, observed:

> The success or failure of a work of art is the responsibility not merely of the creative artist but also of the viewer or reader who perceives his creation. A certain level in the culture of artistic perception is also required of the latter. When our cinema screens are filled with foreign films that teach audiences to perceive the whole world and its contradictions through the prism of love stories, of the personal experiences of the notorious heroes of film melodramas, then it is clear that a film that depicts the masses and that rejects the sentimentalism of individualistic heroes will encounter a certain degree of resistance from an audience that has been reared on different raw material.[116]

Eisenstein's raw material, and his treatment of it above all through montage, and in the case of *October* through emerging notions of *intellectual* montage, are different from mainstream cinema – both as it was then and as it is now. But for cinema as an art form the central question was and remains 'the question of what we can *express cinematically* and how'. To this day it remains a question that very few film-makers have asked, and fewer still with anything like the determination and the cogency that Eisenstein demonstrated in his anniversary film, *October*.

NOTES

· ·

1 Leo Hirsch, 'Ein Musikant ist gestorben'
[A Musician Has Died], *Berliner Tageblatt*,
15 November 1930.

2 Dmitri D. Shostakovich (1906–75) wrote his
first film score for *New Babylon* (directed by
Grigori Kozintsev and Leonid Trauberg, 1929)
and his last for Kozintsev's adaptation of *King
Lear* in 1971. In 1967 he remarked of *October*: 'I
have seen the film, and believe that overall my
music has by and large added to it. But the film
itself does not appeal to me.' I. D. Glickman
(ed.), *Story of a Friendship: The Letters of
Dmitry Shostakorich to Isaak Glickman
1941–1975* (London: Faber, 2001), p. 146.
Sergei S. Prokofiev (1891–1953) collaborated
with Eisenstein on scores for both *Alexander
Nevsky* and *Ivan the Terrible*.

3 As, for instance, in his 'Statement on Sound'
(1928), co-written with Alexandrov and
Vsevolod Pudovkin, translated in Richard
Taylor and Ian Christie (eds), *The Film
Factory: Russian and Soviet Cinema in
Documents, 1896–1939* (hereafter *FF*) (London:
Routledge & Kegan Paul, and Cambridge, MA:
Harvard University Press, 1988), pp. 234–5;
Sergei M. Eisenstein, *Selected Works. Vol. 1:
Writings, 1922–34* (hereafter *ESW 1*) (London:
BFI, and Bloomington: Indiana University
Press, 1988), pp. 113–14; Richard Taylor (ed.),
The Eisenstein Reader (London: BFI, 1998)
(hereafter *ER*), pp. 80–1.

4 From a conversation with the Spanish
writer Alvarez del Vayo cited in Marie Seton,
Sergei M. Eisenstein: A Biography (London:
Dennis Dobson, 1952; revised edn, 1978),
p. 100.

5 For more details of this film, see Richard
Taylor, *The Battleship Potemkin* (London:
I. B. Tauris, 2000).

6 Grigori V. Alexandrov, *Epokha i kino* [The
Epoch and Cinema] (Moscow: Izdatel'stvo
politicheskoi literatury, 1976), pp. 88–9.
Alexandrov's memoirs are full of such
colourful, but regrettably not always reliable,
anecdotes. In many instances, unfortunately,
they provide the only source that we have.

7 See, especially, Mona Ozouf, *Festivals and the
French Revolution* (Cambridge, MA: Harvard
University Press, 1988), chs 2 and 3.

8 Christel Lane, *Rites of Rulers* (Cambridge:
Cambridge University Press, 1981), pp. 2–3.
See also James von Geldern, *Bolshevik
Festivals, 1917–1920* (Berkeley: University of
California Press, 1993), chs 1–3.

9 Anatoli V. Lunacharsky, 'O narodnykh
prazdnestvakh' [On Popular Festivals], *Vestnik
teatra*, 1920, no. 62, 27 April–2 May, cited in:
Vladimir P. Tolstoy, *Agitatsionno-massovoe
iskusstvo: Oformlenie prazdnestv 1917–1932.
Materialy i dokumenty* [Agitational Mass Art:
The Staging of Festivals 1917–1932. Materials
and Documents] (Moscow: Iskusstvo, 1984),
p. 106. Cf. Vladimir Tolstoy, Irina Bibikova
and Catherine Cooke (eds), *Street Art of the
Revolution: Festivals and Celebrations in Russia
1918–33* (London: Thames & Hudson, 1990),
p. 124.

10 Russia did not adopt the Gregorian calendar
until February 1918. By 1917 the discrepancy
between this and the Julian calendar in use then
(and still in use by the Orthodox Church today)
amounted to 13 days, which explains why the
anniversary of 25 October has since been
celebrated on 7 November. Nikolai N. Evreinov
(sometimes also Yevreinov) (1879–1953)
believed in the revitalisation of theatre through
the theatricalisation of life. He emigrated to
France in 1925. *The Storming of the Winter
Palace* is described in von Geldern, pp. 199–207;
Robert Leach, *Revolutionary Theatre* (London
and New York: Routledge, 1994), pp. 46–50;
Konstantin Rudnitsky, *Russian and Soviet
Theatre: Tradition and the Avant-Garde*
(London: Thames & Hudson, 1988), pp. 44–5.

11 Cited in Rudnitsky, p. 44.

12 A. Z. Iufit (ed.), *Russkii sovetkii teatr
1917–1921* [Russian Soviet Theatre 1917–21]
(Leningrad: Iskusstvo, 1968), p. 272.

13 Von Geldern, p. 200.

14 Ibid. Nikolai I. Podvoisky (1880–1948) had
been a member of the Party since 1901 and in
the 1920s was a member of its Central Control
Commission.

15 This was Eisenstein's second abortive
project for a Civil War film. The first had been in
1924, between *The Strike* and *Potemkin*, for a
film version of Isaak Babel's *The Red Cavalry*
short stories: Werner Sudendorf (ed.), *Sergej*

M. Eisenstein: Materialien zu Leben und Werk [Sergei Eisenstein: Materials on His Life and Work] (Munich: Carl Hanser, 1975), pp. 215–16.

16 Cited in Oksana Bulgakowa, *Sergej Eisenstein: Eine Biographie* [Sergei Eisenstein: A Biography] (Berlin: PotemkinPress, 1997), p. 95. Eisenstein was never in fact a member of the Party.

17 Vladimir A. Antonov-Ovseyenko (1884–1939) had returned from exile in Paris in May 1917 and was to play a leading part in the Civil War. However, his sympathies with Trotsky led to an early fall from grace and new exile as Soviet ambassador to Czechoslovakia, Poland and, finally, Spain during the Civil War. Like most Old Bolsheviks, he disappeared during the purges.

18 Cited in Sudendorf, p. 76. Eisenstein made a similar complaint in: 'V boiakh za "Oktiabr"' [In the Struggles for *October*], *Komsomol'skaia pravda*, 2 March 1928.

19 Alexandrov, p. 88.

20 Bulgakowa, p. 95.

21 Ibid.

22 Cited in *FF*, p. 183.

23 Yon Barna, *Eisenstein: The Growth of a Cinematic Genius* (London: Secker & Warburg, 1973), pp. 119–20.

24 Eisenstein, 'V boiakh'.

25 Alexandrov, pp. 92–3.

26 Ibid., p. 94.

27 Ibid., p. 100.

28 This account of the making of the film is based on materials in Bulgakowa, pp. 96–100, Sudendorf, pp. 76–83, and Eisenstein, 'V boiakh'.

29 Alexandrov, pp. 104–5. In fact the fragments of *October* – Lenin's arrival at the Second Congress of the Soviets, the storming of the Winter Palace and the arrest of the Provisional Government – were shown in the Bolshoi's experimental theatre studio. In the main auditorium the audience was able to watch only Pudovkin's *The End of St Petersburg* and Barnet's *Moscow in October* from the list of commissioned anniversary films. The other films had not been finished in time.

30 Grigori V. Alexandrov, *Gody poiskov i truda* [Years of Quest and Toil] (Moscow: Biuro propagandy sovetskogo kinoiskusstva, 1975), p. 32.

31 *Kinogazeta*, 20 December 1927, cited in Jay Leyda, *Kino: A History of the Russian and Soviet Film* (London: George Allen & Unwin, 1960), p. 239.

32 Seton, p. 101.

33 Cited in Bulgakowa, p. 99.

34 Alexandrov, *Epokha*, p. 105.

35 *Blitzzug der Liebe*, also known as *Express Train of Love*, directed by Johannes Guter. This escapist comedy is treated very dismissively in Siegfried Kracauer, *From Caligari to Hitler: A Psychological History of the German Film* (Princeton, NJ: Princeton University Press, 1947), p. 139.

36 Bibliothèque Nationale de France (Arsenal), Fonds Moussinac, no. 008, cited in *Cinémas* (Montréal), Spring 2001, pp. 161–2; cf. the translation in Léon Moussinac, *Sergei Eisenstein: An Investigation into his Films and Philosophy* (New York: Crown Publishers, 1970), p. 28.

37 Léon Moussinac, *Le Cinéma soviétique* (Paris: Gallimard, 1928), p. 161.

38 This footage is included in the video compilation *Moskva: Stranitsy istorii. XX vek* [Moscow: Pages from History. The 20th Century], available from the Museum of the History of the City of Moscow.

39 Vladimir V. Mayakovsky, 'Radovat'sia rano', in Mayakovsky, *Izbrannye proizvedeniia* [Selected Works] (Moscow and Leningrad: Sovetskii pisatel', 1963), vol. 1, pp. 250–1.

40 Sergei M. Eisenstein, *Beyond the Stars: The Memoirs of Sergei Eisenstein* (hereafter *ESW 4*) (Calcutta: Seagull Books, and London: BFI, 1995), pp. 432–3.

41 Dziga Vertov, 'Kinoki. Perevorot', *Lef*, 1923, no. 3 (June/July), pp. 135–43; translated in *FF*, pp. 89–94, this extract on p. 92.

42 The Cathedral was begun in 1839 on the orders of Nicholas I but completed only in 1882 under Alexander III, who attended its consecration. It was destroyed on Stalin's orders in 1931 as part of an anti-religious campaign. It was due to be replaced by the Palace of the Soviets, topped by a huge statue of Lenin, but this could not be built there because the ground was too soggy. The site was then given over to an open-air swimming pool but, since the fall of communism, the Cathedral has been rebuilt, although the statue of Alexander III has not yet reappeared.

43 N. A. Geinike et al. (eds), *Po Moskve* [Around Moscow] (Moscow: M. & S. Sabashnikov, 1917, reprinted Moscow: Izobrazitel'noe iskusstvo, 1991), p. 259.

44 Cited in Rostislav Iurenev, *Sergei Eizenshtein. Zamysli. Fil'my. Metod. Ch. 1: 1898–1929* [Sergei Eisenstein. Projects. Films. Method. Part 1: 1898–1929] (Moscow: Iskusstvo, 1985), p. 223.

45 This remark was recalled in 1925 after Lenin's death by the People's Commissar for Enlightenment, Anatoli Lunacharsky; see *FF*, p. 57.

46 See *FF*, pp. 180–234.

47 See the resolution of the March 1928 Party Conference on Cinema cited in *FF*, p. 210.

48 Eisenstein, 'V boiakh'. This is a reference to the short winter days and consequent lack of daylight, rather than to the parameters of the working day itself.

49 Letter to Alexandrov, 7 August 1927, cited in Alexandrov, *Epokha*, p. 96.

50 Like the other leading Bolsheviks, Vladimir Ulyanov took a pseudonym to protect himself from arrest when working in the political underground.

51 Unlike the red flag that flies on the masthead in *The Battleship Potemkin*, there is no evidence that the flag at the Finland Station was ever coloured red in early performances of *October*.

52 Richard Sakwa (ed.), *The Rise and Fall of the Soviet Union 1917–1991* (London and New York: Routledge, 1999), pp. 33–5.

53 *The Land of Mystery*, released in 1920, was directed by Harold M. Shaw and Basil Thompson and featured an actor called Norman Tharp as Lenoff, a thinly disguised depiction of Lenin.

54 Bulgakowa, p. 94.

55 Alexandrov, *Epokha*, p. 89.

56 On Lenin, see Richard Taylor, *The Politics of the Soviet Cinema 1917–1929* (Cambridge: Cambridge University Press, 1979), p. 54. At the end of *The Fall of Berlin* [Padenie Berlina, dir: Mikhail Chiaureli, 1949–50] Stalin

descends from the heavens like a god and is kissed on the chest by the heroine Natasha as if he were an icon.

57 Alexandrov, *Epokha*, p. 90. Nikandrov's place of origin is given here as Novorossiisk but in the 1983 edition (p. 101n.) Alexandrov changed this to the Urals.

58 Alexandrov, *Epokha*, pp. 90–1 and 101.

59 Cited in Nikolai A. Lebedev, *Ocherk istorii kino SSSR: Nemoe kino (1918–1934)* [An Outline History of the Cinema of the USSR: Silent Cinema (1918–1934)] (Moscow: Iskusstvo, 1965), p. 323.

60 Cited in Iurenev, p. 209.

61 Alexandrov, *Epokha*, p. 101.

62 A. Kamigulov, I. Skorinko, M. Chumandrin, 'Posle *Potemkina – Oktiabr'* plokh' [After *Potemkin – October* is Bad], *Zhizn' iskusstva*, 27 March 1928, p. 12. Ilyich, Lenin's patronymic middle name, is used in Russian as a sign of affection.

63 Nadezhda Krupskaya, 'O fil'me *Oktiabr'*, *Pravda*, 9 February 1928.

64 Viktor Shklovsky, 'Oshibki i izobreteniia' [Mistakes and Inventions], *Novyi Lef*, 1927, nos 11/12, pp. 29–33; translated in *FF*, pp. 180–3, this extract, pp. 182–3.

65 'The Dramaturgy of Film Form (The Dialectical Approach to Film Form)' was originally written in German and is translated in: *ESW1*, pp. 161–80 (this extract on p. 172), and *ER*, pp. 102–3.

66 *ESW4*, pp. 557, 563.

67 '"Eh!" On the Purity of Film Language' (1934), *ESW1*, p. 289; *ER*, p. 128.

68 David Bordwell, *The Cinema of Eisenstein* (Cambridge, MA: Harvard University Press, 1993), p. 88.

69 Iurenev, p. 216.

70 There is a detailed analysis of this sequence in Pierre Sorlin and Marie Claire Ropars, *Octobre: Ecriture et idéologie* (Paris: Editions Albatros, 1976).

71 Kerensky is played by a Leningrad art student called Nikolai Popov, who volunteered his services and was accepted because he suited Eisenstein's typage criteria.

72 Alexandrov, *Epokha*, p. 91.

73 *ESW4*, pp. 315–16.

74 'The Dramaturgy of Film Form' (1929), *ESW 1*, p. 179; *ER*, p. 108.

75 Ibid.

76 The Russian title has the feminine word 'Homeland' [*rodina*] rather than the masculine 'Nation' [*narod*] or the neuter 'Fatherland' [*otechestvo*] to emphasise a particular notion of patriotism and indeed of gender affinity.

77 The Russian title has: 'A democrat on the royal threshold.'

78 Yuri Tsivian, 'Eisenstein and Russian Symbolist Culture: An Unknown Script of *October*' in Ian Christie and Richard Taylor (eds), *Eisenstein Rediscovered* (London and New York: Routledge, 1993), p. 98.

79 Orlando Figes, *A People's Tragedy: The Russian Revolution, 1892–1924* (London: Pimlico, 1997), pp. 426–35.

80 The Russian title makes clear however that this penalty is confined to the military front line.

81 Sakwa, p. 44.

82 See Tsivian, pp. 88–92. In 'Laocoön' Eisenstein described the latter as 'a wooden Chukchi idol': Sergei M. Eisenstein, *Selected Works, Vol. 2: Towards a Theory of Montage* (hereafter *ESW 2*), eds Michael Glenny and Richard Taylor (London: BFI, 1991), p. 117. In a contemporary article he referred to the more primitive representations as 'negro household gods' [*negritianskie penaty*]: Eisenstein, 'V boiakh'.

83 *ESW 1*, pp. 179–80; *ER*, p. 110.

84 'The Principles of the New Russian Cinema' (1930), *ESW 1*, p. 199.

85 Sergei M. Eisenstein, 'From Lectures on Music and Colour in *Ivan the Terrible*', *Selected Works, Vol. 3: Writings, 1934–47* (London: BFI, 1996), p. 331 (hereafter *ESW 3*); *ESW 4*, p. 546.

86 Figes, p. 443.

87 Kornilov was in fact descended from a family of Siberian Cossacks, and the Savage Division was so called because it was composed of native troops from the hill tribes of the Caucasus.

88 Tsivian, pp. 92–5

89 *ESW 3*, pp. 325–6.

90 Although not as obviously as in the original version of Mikhail Romm's *Lenin in October* in which Stalin is clearly Lenin's right-hand man

and is even honoured with the ultimate accolade, 'Comrade Stalin is right'.

91 The Mensheviks, or members of the minority, acquired their name because they were outvoted by the Bolsheviks, or members of the majority, at the 1903 Congress of the Russian Social Democratic Party in London, after which the two factions constituted two separate political groupings. The Mensheviks advocated a more gradual approach to the transition to socialism.

92 In 1917 this room had in fact been used, not by the Mensheviks, but by Trotsky first, and later by Lenin.

93 There is an echo here of Iakov Protazanov's 1914 film *Drama by the Telephone*, a remake of D. W. Griffith's *The Lonely Villa*. In Protazanov's version the telephone also acts as a *failed* medium of communication, informing but not resolving the problem situation depicted on screen. See Richard Taylor and Ian Christie (eds), *Inside the Film Factory: New Approaches to Russian and Soviet Cinema* (London & New York: Routledge, 1991), pp. 9, 52; and Ian Christie and Julian Graffy (eds), *Protazanov and the Continuity of Russian Cinema* (London: BFI, 1993), pp. 64–5.

94 To a British audience the fact that the car is a Rolls-Royce would have had class-related implications. But for a Russian audience this may or may not have been significant. Most contemporary viewers would probably not have known that Lenin also travelled around in a Rolls-Royce! Eisenstein, perhaps surprisingly given his general characterisation of Kerensky, does not make use of the contemporary rumour that the Prime Minister had escaped dressed as a woman, a rumour given currency by the 1920 re-enactment. Alexandrov claimed that they had managed to find the actual car in which Kerensky had escaped: *Epokha*, p. 92.

95 And not, as the English translation has it, 'The Russian Capitol'!

96 'The Dramaturgy of Film Form' (1929), *ESW 1*, p. 177; *ER*, p. 106.

97 Ibid.

98 Tsivian, p. 94.

99 *ESW 4*, pp. 473–4. The tinkling chandeliers came slightly earlier in the sequence of events.

100 *ESW 4*, p. 397.

101 Joanna Bourke, *An Intimate History of Killing* (Cambridge: Granta Books, 1999).

102 *Novyi Lef*, 1928, no. 4 (April), pp. 27–38; translated in *FF*, p. 230.

103 'Montage 1938', *ESW 2*, p. 304.

104 See note 10.

105 Eisenstein, 'V boiakh'.

106 Alexandrov, *Gody*, p. 31.

107 Ibid., p. 32.

108 'Images of a Revolution', *Timewatch*, BBC 2, 14 October 1987.

109 *Novyi Lef*, 1928, no. 4 (April), pp. 27–38; translated in *FF*, p. 230.

110 'Through the Revolution to Art' (1933), *ESW 1*, p. 244.

111 'The Principles of the New Russian Cinema' (1930), *ESW 1*, p. 197.

112 See the remarks made on this subject by Viktor Shklovsky, Esfir Shub and Osip Brik, translated in *FF*, pp. 183, 217 and 227.

113 'Beyond the Shot' (1929), *ESW 1*, p. 142; *ER*, p. 85.

114 From a 1936 article cited in 'On Colour', *ESW 2*, p. 265.

115 'Beyond the Played and the Non-Played' (1928), *ESW 1*, p. 105; *ER*, pp. 78–9.

116 '*Oktiabr*' – (Itogi diskussii)' [*October* – The Results of the Discussion], *Zhizn' iskusstva*, 27 May 1928, translated in *FF*, pp. 232–5, this extract p. 233.

CREDITS

. . . .

October

USSR
1928

Production Studio
Sovkino (Moscow and
Leningrad)
**Directors and
Scriptwriters**
Sergei M. Eisenstein, Grigori
V. Alexandrov
Assistant Directors
Maxim M. Strauch, Mikhail
Gomorov, Ilya Z. Trauberg
Cinematographer
Eduard K. Tisse
Camera Assistants
Vladimir Popov, Vladimir S.
Nilsen
Sets
Vasili I. Kovrigin

Cast
Vasili N. Nikandrov
Lenin
Nikolai Popov
Kerensky
Boris N. Livanov
Tereshchenko, a minister in
the Provisional Government
Sokolov
Vladimir A. Antonov-
Ovseyenko
Nikolai I. Podvoisky
Himself
Lyashchenko
Konovalov
Chibisov
Skobelev
Mikholev
Kishkin
Smelsky
Verderevsky
Sailor Ognev
Himself – the sailor who
fired the signal from the
Aurora
Eduard K. Tisse
A German officer

Leningrad workers, Red
Army soldiers, sailors from
the Baltic Fleet of the Red
Navy

9,317 feet
2,800 metres
Black and White

**First private screening of
extracts**
7 November 1927
First private screenings
14 and 23 January 1928,
Moscow
Public premières
14 March 1928

Sound version
USSR
1967

Production Studio
Mosfilm
Director
Grigori V. Alexandrov
Music
From the works of Dmitri D.
Shostakovich

Credits checked by
Markku Salmi,
BFI Filmographic Unit

BIBLIOGRAPHY

· ·

EISENSTEIN'S WRITINGS

The Eisenstein Reader (London: BFI, 1998).

Selected Works, Volume 1: Writings, 1922–34 (London: BFI, 1988).

Selected Works, Volume 2: Towards a Theory of Montage (London: BFI, 1991).

Selected Works, Volume 3: Writings, 1934–47 (London: BFI, 1996)

Selected Works, Volume 4: Beyond the Stars: The Memoirs of Sergei Eisenstein (Calcutta: Seagull Books, and London: BFI, 1995).

There is no reliable version of the film script available in English.

OTHERS ON EISENSTEIN AND *OCTOBER*

Aumont, Jacques, *Montage Eisenstein* (London: BFI, and Bloomington: Indiana University Press, 1987).

Barna, Yon, *Eisenstein: The Growth of a Cinematic Genius* (London: Secker & Warburg, and Bloomington: Indiana University Press, 1973).

Bordwell, David, *The Cinema of Eisenstein* (Cambridge, MA: Harvard University Press, 1993).

Bulgakowa, Oksana, *Sergej Eisenstein: Eine Biographie* (Berlin: PotemkinPress, 1997).

Goodwin, James, *Eisenstein: Cinema and History* (Urbana: University of Illinois Press, 1993).

Iurenev, Rostislav, *Sergei Eizenshtein. Zamysli. Fil'my. Metod. Ch. 1: 1898–1929* (Moscow: Iskusstvo, 1985).

Leyda, Jay, *Kino: A History of the Russian and Soviet Film* (London: George Allen & Unwin, 1960).

Moussinac, Léon, *Sergei Eisenstein: An Investigation into his Films and Philosophy* (New York: Crown Publishers, 1970).

Seton, Marie, *Sergei M. Eisenstein: A Biography* (London: Dennis Dobson, 1952; revised edn, 1978).

Sorlin, Pierre, and Marie Claire Ropars, *Octobre: Ecriture et idéologie* (Paris: Editions Albatros, 1976).

Taylor, Richard, and Ian Christie (eds), *The Film Factory: Russian and Soviet Cinema in Documents, 1896–1939* (London: Routledge & Kegan Paul, and Cambridge, MA: Harvard University Press, 1988).

Tsivian, Yuri, 'Eisenstein and Russian Symbolist Culture: An Unknown Script of *October*', in Ian Christie and Richard Taylor (eds), *Eisenstein Rediscovered* (London and New York: Routledge, 1993).

ALSO PUBLISHED

If you would like further
information about future
BFI Film Classics or about
other books on film, media
and popular culture from
BFI Publishing, please
write to:

BFI Film Classics
BFI Publishing
21 Stephen Street
London W1P 2LN

BFI FILM

CLASSICS

BFI Film Classics '...could scarcely be improved upon ... informative, intelligent, jargon-free companions.'
The Observer

Each book in the BFI Publishing Film Classics series honours a great film from the history of world cinema. With new titles published each year, the series is rapidly building into a collection representing some of the best writing on film. If you would like to receive further information about future Film Classics or about other books on film, media and popular culture from BFI Publishing, please fill in your name and address and return this card to the BFI.* (No stamp required if posted in the UK, Channel Islands, or Isle of Man.)

NAME

ADDRESS

POSTCODE

WHICH *BFI FILM CLASSIC* DID YOU BUY?

* In North America, please return your card to: Indiana University Press, Attn: LPB, 601 N. Morton Street, Bloomington, IN 47401-3797

BFI Publishing
21 Stephen Street
FREEPOST 7
LONDON
W1E 4AN